MW00769108

THE OUTTRAVELER

HAWAII

MATTHEW LINK

alyson books
NEW YORK

THIS TRADE PAPERBACK ORIGINAL IS PUBLISHED BY

Alyson Books

245 West 17th Street

New York, New York 10011

DISTRIBUTION IN THE UNITED KINGDOM BY

Turnaround Publisher Services Ltd.

Unit 3, Olympia Trading Estate

Coburg Road, Wood Green

London N22 6TZ England.

FIRST EDITION: *April 2008*

08 09 10 11 12   a   10 9 8 7 6 5 4 3 2 1

ISBN-10 1-59350-073-3

ISBN-13 978-1-59350-073-3

Library of Congress Cataloging-in-Publication data are on file

Design by VICTOR MINGOVITS

Maps by MATTHEW LINK

As the editor in chief of The Out Traveler, *I'm delighted at the launch of our new travel series.* The Out Traveler *strives to inspire sophisticated readers like you by showcasing thoughtful and transformative travel experiences that set the standard of gay travel. These books, which emphasize the long-overlooked, but incredibly powerful cultural and historical traditions of our community throughout the world, help us reach this goal.*

—ED SALVATO
EDITOR IN CHIEF, *The Out Traveler*
CORPORATE DIRECTOR OF TRAVEL MEDIA
AT PLANETOUT INC.

ABOUT THE AUTHOR

Matthew Link is the Editor at Large of *The Out Traveler* magazine (published by *The Advocate* and *OUT*). Link lived on the Big Island of Hawaii for five years, and published the first-ever gay and lesbian guidebook to Hawaii during his residence there. Destined to be a travel writer, Link grew up on his father's 52-foot sailboat during his teenage years, cruising around Southeast Asia and the Pacific with his father's girlfriend and her two teenage daughters—a time in his life he has written about in the story "The Unquenchable Sea," which won Best Memoir in a contest sponsored by Travelers' Tales. Link has also called Hong Kong, the Philippines, Micronesia, Papua, New Guinea, and New Zealand home—as well as traveling to 60 countries and Antarctica. He worked personally for Arthur Frommer, the founder of the first modern guidebook series, at Frommer's magazine *Budget Travel*. Link has also written travel pieces for *Newsweek*, *Time Asia*, *Forbes*, *Men's Health*, *Men's Fitness*, *Real Simple*, and Web sites such as, MSNBC.com, Concierge.com, and many others. His travel stories have been published in numerous anthology books, including *Between the Palms* and *Wonderlands*. Link has also been a video documentary maker, producing a number of socially themed award-winning documentaries that played in numerous international film festivals and on PBS stations. Link's favorite destination in the world is Africa, which he has visited seven times. He is an avid kayaker, hiker, snowboarder, and skin diver.

THE OUT TRAVELER PHILOSOPHY

Yes, we know: On your travels around the globe (or even close to home), you've plowed through your fair share of dry, Yellow Page-like guidebooks aimed at the most massive of mass markets. Sure, they may include a tiny gay section that makes a token nod to you, but little else. Moreover, many guides seem to rely so heavily on throwing as much soon-to-be-outdated information at you, that you are left wondering about the deeper aspects of a place. How is it unique from others? What's it like to live there? How is being gay there different from other places? What are the more meaningful things I need to know to really understand where I'm going?

Our vision with this guidebook is born from the same desire we share with *The Out Traveler* magazine. We aim to give you the expert tools that will not only lend practicality to your journey, but also cultural and historical insight, understanding, and intimate appreciation of where you're going—and of course, how to do it all in style.

THE LGBT TRAVELER

Loosened from the bonds of tradition and societal expectations, gay and lesbian people have been trailblazers throughout human history. And it's no different with our distinctive take on travel. Queer people have frequently had to sojourn to distant shores to find our true "homes." We often understand a place and discover its layers years before our heterosexual comrades do. As the globe opens up even further in the 21st century to welcome us, offering more places than ever for the LGBT traveler to visit, we still need to explore the world with our eyes wide open. Perhaps it's part of our special survival skill set: Queer people have to know where we are welcome, how to fit in, the vibe of a particular cultural or political climate—all things many straights take for granted. In a word, we are savvy. And innovative. And our authors strive to reflect that innate intelligence in our guidebooks. We want to impart to you the travel tools for deeper understanding. After all, even the slightest of vacations is meant to be transformative.

THE OUT TRAVELER GUIDES

Instead of throwing in the kitchen sink, we present you with our knowledgeable hand picked recommendations. We cull, interview, visit, and delve deeply to find both the gay and mainstream establishments we feel fit well with sophisticated queer sensibility, with an emphasis on the luxurious, the classy, or at least the truly unique. You'll also find call-outs throughout the book that direct you to our Web site, OutTraveler.com, which loads more up-to-the-minute articles, listings, and information on a particular locale can be found. In our *Out Traveler* guidebooks, we spend time exploring the distinct history, politics, and the unexpected quirks of a place in order for you to become a sharp traveler, not just a fly-by-night tourist. If we can illuminate a locale's soul for you, then we have done our job.

No establishment has paid to be in our guides—you are getting our often-opinionated take on what we feel is worthwhile. Our authors are personally involved in the places they write about, often having resided in the destination for years. Nothing beats local, on-the-ground, insider expertise. Our authors give you pertinent knowledge on local laws and attitudes toward gays in our signature *Out Traveler* ratings boxes found in every chapter. For the record, in Hawaii our inexpensive lodgings are up to roughly $120 a night, moderate lodgings from roughly $120 to $200 a night, and expensive lodgings are $200+ a night. Similar categories for restaurant meals are budget up to $12, moderate from $12 to $20, and expensive $20+.

So sit back and let us take you on a trip. Travel is profoundly personal and frequently life changing. Let us help you discover the essence of what the journey is all about.

—MATTHEW LINK
EDITOR AT LARGE, *The Out Traveler* MAGAZINE

CONTENTS

CHAPTER 4

 NEW YORK CITY WEB LINKS AND TIPS ON OUTTRAVELER.COM

HAWAII AND ME

I grew up in the Tropics. In places with exotic and obscure names like Palau, Vanuatu, New Caledonia, Papua, New Guinea. Lapping waves, molasses-like humidity, sleepy villages, and even malaria were all very familiar to me. After years living as an adult in California, I decided it was time for my boyfriend and I to escape, and for me to return to my natural setting of outstretched palm trees, black sand beaches, and mysterious mountains. We chose the most foreign place we could find while still technically remaining in the U.S. We ended up on the Kona coast of the Big Island of Hawaii.

For years, we lived on the steep slope of Mauna Kea, overlooking the endless Pacific from our cliff-side perch. Hardened lava flows flanked us on either side, and my kayak rested on the pebble beach just a ten-minute walk from our home. Wild goats and boars lived in the nearby forests, and all the while, the mystical presence of Pele, the beloved yet malevolent volcano goddess, seemed to be hovering in the distance.

I tell you all this to paint the picture of the almost mythical nature of the 50th state we call Hawaii. It's not just residents who tap into this vibe—talk to any tourist who travels over thousands of miles of open ocean to plop down on one of her beaches, and they know the same thing. There is something amorphous about the place, like it exists in its own reality. Sure, you may have to look past the drive-through fast food joints, the traffic, the concrete resorts, and the high-rises that crowd Waikiki. But you don't have to look far. Hawaii always remains uniquely magical.

Gays have always had a special connection to Hawaii. After all, the place is known for its tolerance, its way of "aloha," and its stunning beauty that appeals to the queer aesthetic. Men wear flowers in their hair, women can be strong, and even ancient Hawaiian culture revered the "third sex" of the *mahu*. I now reside in Hawaii's antithesis, a crazy place called New York City, but not a week goes by where I don't experience a vivid dream about Hawaii. I can smell the plumeria, feel the trade winds, and touch the soft sand. No wonder I am constantly drawn back to her shores, and once I've made the journey back, I feel like I never left. Hawaii does that you. It gets under your skin and never really lets go.

Hawaii is not like other places. Rules of far away continents don't apply or translate here. Hawaii is her own, surrounded by thousands of miles of colossal ocean, proudly peaking up above the horizon like a hidden child. As with most foreign lands, the traveler must take her on her own terms. You'll find Polynesia here, as well as America and Asia and many other places. But they are all guests in the land. The islands themselves are strong and perpetual, and have their own true song. Listen carefully and reverently. You'll hear it.

—MATT LINK

THE OUT TRAVELER

HAWAII

UNDERSTANDING HAWAIIAN HISTORY AND POLITICS FOR THE OUT TRAVELER

HOMOSEXUALITY
IN HAWAIIAN HISTORY

Although most information about pre-contact Hawaii was written after contact and thus shaded by the bias of foreigners, Hawaiians have a strong heritage of *mele* or chants that explain the olden times. It seems sexuality in old Hawaiian culture was treated as a loving, fluid part of everyday life. Like in the Psalms, it had a poetic characteristic. In the *hula* and *mele* you can still witness the exquisite form of sensuality that was part of a people who celebrated their sexuality. In fact, Hawaiians named their genitals as a matter of course. There were also *mele ma'i*, or songs in honor of genitals, performed at events like the birth of a great chief.

Hawaiian family structures are and were collective and extended, unlike nuclear mom-and-pop Mainland families. Many related and unrelated aunties, uncles, cousins, and *hanai* (adopted) family members merge together as an *ohana*. According to tradition, the first-born was often given to the grandparents or others to raise. Mates were merely given the poetic label of *noho* ai, or "one to lay with." Private property in terms of marriage was unheard of. Although family lines were blurred in this way, genealogy was of utmost importance to the Hawaiians. Many old chants are solely information on lineage.

Old Hawaiian society was a class system, and the *Alii*, or royalty, were believed to be directly descended from the gods. Thus, they had great *mana* or spiritual power. The bones of the *Alii* were always hidden after death to preserve this *mana*. The commoners, or *makaainana*, were the farmers and fisherman and everyday workers, while the *kauwa* or slave class were marked by specific facial tattoos. The *kauwa* class was only allowed to live in certain designated areas. As you can guess, they were the ones routinely used for human sacrifices at the temples of the war god, Kuka'ilimoku, but never thrown into fiery volcanoes as Hollywood would like you to believe!

AIKANE: MORE THAN GOOD FRIENDS

Many say that old Hawaii was neither purely a heterosexual nor homosexual, but a bisexual culture. Same-sex relationships were evidently frequent, and many men and women had *aikane* or *punahele*: close friends or "favorites" that were at times involved sexually. No particular shame was associated with same-gender sex at all, and sodomy was not considered wrong. The words *hookamaka* and *moe aikane* were common terms used to denote same-sex relations. (They were obviously years ahead in politically correct terminology!) The more explicit way to put it was *upi laho*, which translates to something like testicle pressing, or literally "scrotum squirting."

The word *aikane* itself relates to a particular sexual relationship in old Hawaii. It is a combination of *ai*, meaning to have sex with, and *kane*, meaning man. *Aikane* nowadays is used to mean "good friends," and most people don't realize what the word actually once pertained to.

Aikane relationships between men in old Hawaii are only recorded among the *Alii* and high chiefs, but probably occurred between commoners as well. Royal *aikane* seemed to have been a whole rank of people who were granted special political and social status as a result of a sexual role (like Monica Lewinsky?). Since the high *Alii* had an obligation to mate with certain other royals, *aikane* were chosen voluntarily out of desire rather than duty. They were kept as exclusive concubines to the chiefs. Most *aikane* rose up from the lower ranks of royalty, and their sexual friendships with higher *Alii* increased their *mana* and power.

Although *aikane* were usually young male sexual companions to the *Alii*, they often had their own wives and children, and were not seen as less masculine in any way. *Aikane* relationships didn't seem to be regulated by any "top or bottom" order, regardless of age or ranking. There were also female *aikane* (the word often occurs in the Pele goddess stories), but since women were subjugated in many aspects of society, it made for a stronger "guys only" club of royal *aikane* relationships that disregarded many women folk.

The *aikane* role seems to have been honorable and noble, and was not hidden at all. In fact, it was even boasted about to shocked European sailors. *Aikane* relations were talked about freely and often in Hawaiian culture, since they were an important part of the royal hierarchy. These homosexual relationships had social value, and there are even ancient stories referring to *aikane* living together in great sacredness.

The first Europeans to set eyes on Hawaii were aboard Captain Cook's vessel in 1779 (although there's historical evidence that Spaniards "discovered" the islands as early as 1627). When he first appeared, Cook was mistaken for the god Lono, but later he and the sailors showed themselves up for the mere humans they were.

The ship journals during this voyage described a culture that was

THE DEAD SPEAK

Certain eyebrow-raising passages from the journals of
Captain Cook's expedition have long been overlooked by
heterosexual scholars. In the early 1990s, Robert J. Morris
made a concerted study of the logs from the ships *Discovery*
and *Resolution*, which revealed some interesting tidbits on
old Hawaiian culture. Among the juicy samples, drenched in
eighteenth century views of decency:

From the log of David Samwell, ship's surgeon, 29th of
January, 1779:

"Of this Class [aikane] are Parea [Palea] and Cani-
Coah [Kanekoa] and their business is to commit
the Sin of Onan upon the old King. This, however
strange it may appear, is fact, as we learnt from the
frequent Enquiries about this curious Custom, and
it is an office that is esteemed honourable among
them & they have frequently asked us on seeing
a handsome young fellow if he was not an Ikany
[aikane] to some of us."

ambiguously bisexual to Western eyes. Cook's men wrote aghast
accounts of close, brotherly *aikane* relationships within the *Alii*—
"a shocking inversion of the laws of nature, they bestow all those
affections upon them that were intended for the other sex" as one
of the sailors put it. They recorded the kings of Maui, Kauai, and

THE DEAD SPEAK

From the log of Charles Clerke, second in command, March, 1779:

> "...every Aree [alii] according to his rank keeps so many women and so many young men (Icarnies [aikane] as they call them) for the amusement of his leisure hours; they talk of this infernal practice with all the indifference in the world, nor do I suppose they imagine any degree of infamy in it."

From Samwell's log of the 10th of February, 1779:

> "He [Kamehameha] with many of his attendants took up quarters on board the ship for the Night: among them is a Young Man of whom he seems very fond, which does not in the least surprise us, as we have had opportunities before of being acquainted with a detestable part of his Character which he is not in the least anxious to conceal."

the Big Island all having their own *aikane*. There's even one account of chief Kalanikoa of Kauai asking if a certain young handsome European sailor would become his personal *aikane* for a little while, and he offered six valuable hogs to boot! It wasn't recorded if the lad said yes (but for six pigs, you decide!).

Although heterosexual historians don't like to mention it, the sailors' journals also record that the great unitor of the Hawaiian Islands, the famous King Kamehameha, brought aboard one young *aikane* while traveling on Cook's ship. According to tradition, some children were raised specifically to become *aikane* of the chief. Scholars figure the king also had male *aikane* in his household (in addition to his two wives and numerous courtesan women—what a stud!), as well as intimate *aikane* relationships with high-ranking male ministers.

In fact, some scholars profess that Kamehameha himself was a "favorite" of King Kalaniopuu. There are sketchy details of a jealous rivalry between Kamehameha and another of the King's *aikane*, Palea, which ended in Kamehameha's favor. The trouble-making Palea is often credited with setting up a theft incident during Cook's stay in Kealakekua Bay on the Big Island. The incident led to mistrust between the formerly neighborly Europeans and Hawaiians, and finally led to Cook's attempt to kidnap King Kalaniopuu for ransom of the stolen boat. A large skirmish ensued and Cook was beaten and stabbed to death in the conflict.

Cook's death didn't stop other European voyages to Hawaii, including Captain Vancouver's. The knowledge of war technology that the outsiders brought was closely studied by Kamehameha. He eventually took control of the Big Island and conquered the entire island chain by brute force.

Did the fabled king have any sexual preference, or was he merely following old Hawaiian customs by having *aikane*? We'll probably never know. For Hawaiians, it's an irrelevant point, since these kinds of sexual lines have little meaning or purpose. But the *aikane* tradition didn't end with King Kamehameha. Historical rumor has it that his grandson, King Kamehameha III (1815–1854), had his own *aikane* too.

YOUR MAJESTY

The Hawaiians' fondness for naming their genitals wasn't limited to the commoners: it's been said that King Kalakaua's penis had the impressive name of *halala* (literally translated as *to bend low*), and Queen Liliuokalani's vagina was called *anapau* (which means frisky).

MAHU: DUDE LOOKS LIKE A LADY

Besides the tradition of *aikane*, another notable queer aspect of the Hawaiian culture is the *mahu*. Transvestism was, and still is, frequent in parts of Polynesia, where men choose to don women's apparel, grow up as a girl, and even become a wife of another man, perhaps one of several, sometimes even cutting his/her thighs to "menstruate." Some traditions tell of a male, usually a younger brother, being compelled to take on the feminine role of family caretaker and keeper of traditions when a suitable daughter is lacking. *Mahu* in old Hawaii referred to either an effeminate male or a masculine female, someone who took on the opposite gender's role. Whether or not that meant homosexuality was not important, they held a necessary role in the *ohana* and were not outcasts.

Nowadays the word *mahu* usually refers to a local male transvestite or an effeminate man, who is primarily gay and non-white. At times it's also used simply to mean any gay man. *Mahu* is now seldom used for women, and there seems to be no Hawaiian word for lesbian.

Despite aspects of an *ohana*, inclusive society, pre-contact Hawaii was still a vigorous and potent culture. Society was strictly regimented by the *Alii* in the form of *kapu* (taboo) laws. For instance,

UNDERSTANDING HAWAIIAN HISTORY AND POLITICS FOR THE OUT TRAVELER stepping on the king's shadow was grounds for execution, as was failing to kneel or prostrate in his presence. *Kapu* laws, however arbitrary, kept everyone in check and the often-warring chief's societies running somewhat smoothly.

Interestingly, the fall and winter months were usually designated as a time of peace and planting, with wars commencing after February. It's been said that *mahu* were sometimes encouraged to follow the warriors into battle; not to fight, but to fill the female role while the men were away from their homes for so long.

Women often had same-sex relations while men were away at war. There are also accounts of women sometimes taking on the traditional male role of warrior and accompanying their men in battle. These Hawaiian Amazons were called *wahine kaua*, or battle women. They asked to be warriors, and the men obligingly trained them in this traditionally masculine occupation. They were seen as nothing terribly unordinary, and they would return to their family life after war.

Between men and women, there were many *kap* laws and social mores. Women couldn't fish or even touch men's fishing equipment. Women couldn't eat certain kinds of fish, pork, coconuts, or even bananas. Women had it tough no doubt—the only compensation being that older women were looked upon very highly. They could become honorary *kupuna* or elders, setting down the laws of a region. Some recorded rare instances tell of women being given the male role of priest from birth and becoming *na kaula wahine*, or women-prophets.

Some specific *kapu* may have worked to the homo's advantage. One edict was that after seven or eight years of age, men could only sleep in the men's house while women slept in the women's house. King Kamehameha himself practiced this law. Men and women couldn't even eat together, only with members of the same

THE PEN IS MIGHTIER

In 1963, the *Honolulu Advertiser* ran a three-part article entitled "The Deviate," about the growing problem of homosexuality in the community. In 1964, there was an article about transvestites and the people who liked to watch them. Reference was made to a law passed that same year that required all men dressed as women to wear a card that said "I'm a boy" or "I'm a male." In 1967, there was another article about "The Strange World of Oahu's Different People," and in 1968 a piece about Hawaii's so-called loneliest citizens: "Mahus Are People, Too." It wasn't until 1969 that the paper finally relented and ran a more positive article that suggested homosexuality was actually natural for some people.

sex (talk about bonding!). However, there are occasional accounts of apparently *mahu* men being allowed to eat and sleep with the women as one of them.

The eating *kapu* was finally abolished when King Kamehameha II sat down for some royal "grinds" with his mother, Queen Ka'ahumanu, in 1819, effectively ending the whole *kapu* system altogether. It's speculated the strong-willed queen wanted to crush the powerful *kahuna* or priest class in the process.

With the fall of the *kapu* system and the coincidental arrival of missionaries shortly after in 1820, many old customs slowly became extinct. Although it's easy to pick on the oppressive missionaries for the obvious destruction they inflicted upon the Hawaiian culture (not to mention the custom of wearing lots of clothes!), the good ones did set up hospitals and schools for the islanders.

They also helped create the first Hawaiian alphabet and written language. Their adversaries, the whalers, made prostitutes out of the women and displayed less concern for the native born. Of interest, Hawaiian beliefs and Christianity somewhat overlap. The Hawaiian creation myth closely mirrors the one in Genesis. The Hawaiians also believed in a great god Lono who would return to Earth, and in the loving and forgiving high god Kane, to whom all life was sacred.

During this time of cultural upheaval, many *mahu* were involved in carrying on the outlawed hula dance and chants clandestinely. Even today, many gay men are *kumu hula* (mentors of hula) and hula dancers, and are respected for their talents and creative abilities. As always, the queers keep the arts and culture alive throughout history!

HOMO HAWAII POLITICS
GOING TO THE CHAPEL

Hawaii is seen as an amazingly open and liberal state, which it often is and sometimes isn't. Since it was the first state to legalize abortion and ratify the Equal Rights Amendment, Hawaii seems like a natural environment for the legalization of same-gender civil marriages. The irony is that Hawaii has a fairly politically indifferent gay community, rural and traditionalist voters statewide, and an island culture that discourages forwardness and "boat-rocking." Add to this the federal backlash against same-sex marriage, and you can see why the road has been a long and bumpy one, filled with enormous blocks.

The whole legal same-gender marriage movement in the U.S. began in December of 1990, when three homo couples (two lesbian and one male) applied for marriage licenses at the Honolulu City Hall. They were—you guessed it—denied a couple months later.

Attorney Dan Foley filed a suit on their behalf, which became known as the Baehr vs. Miike case.

The case was ultimately appealed to the State Supreme Court, which ruled in favor of the gay couples in 1993. In the court's opinion, the state was refusing to grant marriage licenses (and thus marriage rights) due to the gender of couples applying. Technically, the sexual orientation of the couples had nothing to do with it. The Hawaii State Constitution is probably the most human rights oriented state constitution in the U.S., and strongly prohibits discrimination based on gender.

Although this amazing ruling was handed back down to a lower court and did not become law, it made headline news around the globe. Thus began the backlash against "Hawaii's gay marriages." State legislatures across the U.S. scrambled to pass laws and change constitutions limiting marriage to one man and one woman. And of course, Bill Clinton signed the Defense of Marriage Act in 1996 to make sure no one would have to recognize what little Hawaii had done. Or what everybody thought it had done.

In retaliation to the Supreme Court's 1993 ruling, the Hawaii legislature abruptly passed Act 217 in the spring of 1994. The act asserted that procreation was the basis for marriage. This was despite the fact that procreation had been taken out of the statute in 1984 as discriminatory against the elderly and disabled. The act was widely understood as ineffective and unconstitutional. Two other attempts to amend the state constitution were killed in legislative committees.

One interesting thing that Act 217 did was to create a Commission on Sexual Orientation and the Law. The commission looked at marriage rights and privileges, heard public testimony, and examined many witnesses. In late 1995, after studying the overwhelming evidence, the commission recommended full marriage benefits for same-gender couples.

In late 1996, when the ball was relayed into his lower court, Judge Kevin Chang finally ruled that there was no compelling state interest in not issuing marriage licenses to same-gender couples. That monumental decision technically allowed same-gender marriage in Hawaii. But of course the state's Department of Health refused to issue licenses. Judge Chang granted a stay, which meant it went back to the State Supreme Court.

In the meantime, a very watered down form of same-sex marriage was passed on July 1, 1997, called the Reciprocal Beneficiaries Act. It gave only 60 out of 400 benefits that married people enjoy. The license is technically a legal document between two unmarried people (a mother and son could get one). It covers important areas of insurance, worker's compensation, hospital visits, survivorship rights, and survivorship benefits. And it must be said it is better than what other U.S. states have. However, in actual usage, the R.B. Act has proven to be quite toothless, with many challenging its very function. Many say the license is not worth the paper it's written on.

One thing that appeals to Mainland gays is the fact that one does not need to be a resident to obtain an "R.B." license. It could also prove beneficial for insurance policies and estate planning in other states. Regardless of all the legal this and that's, gays have been flocking to Hawaii for years to get "married" anyway, and many island business are set up primarily for executing your fabulously illegal same-gender union.

The State Supreme Court was expected to rule on Judge Chang's verdict in favor of gays in early 1998. This would have been the final ruling and whatever the outcome, it would stick. The Hawaii Supreme Court, who has already ruled in favor once, would have no choice but to abide and allow same-gender couples the right to marry. However, The Supreme Court held off on its ruling. It was decided that this sensitive civil rights issue should go to unprecedented popular statewide vote in November instead. The results were disastrous.

Mainland money on both sides of the issue began pouring into normally politically demure Hawaii. The group Save Traditional Marriage began their assault on local media with distasteful TV and print ads, including one with mock tourists explaining why they won't visit Hawaii if it passes. Another showed a child reading a same-gender marriage book and asking disturbing questions. Protect Our Constitution, on the other hand, was criticized for linking the issue to abortion and sweeping the homosexual aspects of the issue under the rug. Sign-waving along Hawaii's streets, a quaint island tradition during election time, at times turned into ugly yelling matches. This was the land of aloha?

Hawaii voters defeated same-sex marriage by a landslide (68% to 32%). Many island gays and lesbians who had long felt safe and sound in tolerant Hawaii began to question their stand on the islands. Conservative groups announced a victory of common sense and denounced those who called them "homophobic." Queer tourists thought twice about their next vacation.

Why did the vote go the way it did? It could have been the strong political presence of the Mormon and Catholic churches on the islands, the elderly age of the average voter, or the fact that Hawaii had fought with the marriage issue for so long that even liberal voters grew tired of it. Or it could have been that same-sex marriage was just too radical for modest Hawaii to tackle.

In 1999, Governor Ben Cayetano dedicated himself to passing a strong domestic partnership bill in place of gay marriage (although it would not include adoption or custody rights). But in 2001, bill HB 1468 Relating to Civil Unions finally died without ever receiving a hearing in the House Judiciary Committee. In February

GETTING' HITCHED, HAWAIIAN STYLE

When Hawaii led the charge for same-sex marriage in the U.S. in the early '90s, a number of gay and lesbian wedding services sprouted. Almost every one offers beach or tropical garden ceremonies, Hawaiian ministers, and traditions like conch shell blowing and hula, helicopter or horseback riding, or other excursions. Some can help with accommodations as well. Since there is much hope that gay marriage will actually pass soon in the state, now's the time to book your fabulous gay wedding in paradise:

ALOHA MAUI GAY WEDDINGS
(888) 822-9700
ALOHAMAUIGAYWEDDINGS.COM

A RAINBOW IN PARADISE
(808) 372-0343
ARAINBOWINPARADISE.COM

GAY WEDDINGS HAWAII STYLE
(888) 583-9529
KAMELE.COM

2003, another civil unions bill lost by one vote in the legislature.

One LGBT victory was the signing in June 2001 of a Hawaii hate crimes bill, by Lt. Governor Hirono, who, as a legislator, helped introduce previous hate crimes bills. She signed instead of Governor Cayetano, who at one point threatened to veto the bill (despite it

1

GETTING' HITCHED, HAWAIIAN STYLE

HAWAII GAY WEDDINGS
(800) 659-1866, (808) 875-8569
HAWAIIANGAYWEDDINGS.COM

HOLY UNION COMMITMENT CEREMONIES
(808) 821-1690

1 & 1 WEDDING BY THE SEA
(808) 942-7772
WEDDINGBYTHESEA-HAWAII.COM/
GAYCEREMONY.HTM

GAY HAWAII WEDDINGS
(808) 235-6966
GAYHAWAIIWEDDINGS.NET

UNIONS IN PARADISE
(866) 662-2661
UNIONSINPARADISE.COM

passing both the House and Senate by overwhelming majorities), quipping "This is not the kind of place where you see gay people beaten up, killed, or ostracized." This comment was made just days before an attack on a camp outing by a local gay group on Kauai, and a public uproar convinced the Governor to change his mind and allow passage of the bill. In April 2003, the term "gender identity and expression" was added to the Hate Crime Law.

Fast forward to January 2007, when not one, not two, but three bills pertaining to same-sex marriage were introduced in the state legislature: two in the House (HB 907 and HB 908) and one in the Senate (SB 1062). Each bill was introduced as free-standing in its own right and is not dependant upon any other. Since Hawaii law allows gay partners various rights such as family and bereavement leaves, probate rights, and hospital visitation, the main benefits derived from a new civil-union status would be rights governing areas such as taxation and adoption.

There was so much support for the new bills that even Debi Hartmann, the former director of a group that formed to stop same-sex marriage in Hawaii, Hawaii Future Today, semi-supported HB 908. "One of the things this civil union bill does not impact is the current marriage language," she said.

It all sounded like great news for civil unions to finally pass in Hawaii, but unfortunately the first bill to get a hearing, Civil Unions bill (HB 908), was deferred indefinitely (which some saw as its death) in the House Judiciary Committee after more than five hours of passionate testimony by local gays and lesbians. The deferment happened despite the fact that the Gay, Lesbian, Bisexual, and Transgendered Caucus for the Hawaii Democratic Party survey of legislators discovered that the majority of state elected officials supported civil unions.

"It was going to die," said Committee Chairman Tommy Waters, who was rumored to have close ties with the Catholic opponents of the bill. "It would have died at the table so rather than killing the measure I deferred the bill. The bill is still alive, so I'm encouraging the LGBT Caucus and the other side to come back to the table and let's work out a compromise. Let's talk about what rights are being denied and let's provide them."

So is there still hope for gay marriage in Hawaii? It has yet to be seen. Senate Judiciary Chairman Clayton Hee says he won't schedule a hearing on Senate Bill 1062, which would grant civil unions the full legal rights of married couples, unless it appears likely the measure also would fly in the House. The fate of HB 907 is yet undetermined. These things happen slowly in Hawaii, so don't expect a firm outcome anytime soon.

THE LONG HARD ROAD TO HUMAN RIGHTS

Homosexual acts done in private were decriminalized in Hawaii in the early '70s. In 1975, Hawaii's first homosexual protection bill was introduced in the state legislature. It was passed by the House but rejected by the Senate. In 1977, it was reintroduced but died in committee, and in 1978 a gay rights amendment to the state constitution was also killed. The first gay rights law wasn't until 1992, in the form of a law prohibiting job discrimination based on sexual orientation finally passed by the state legislature (and it was about time!). In 2001, Hawaii became the 26th state to pass a hate crimes bill covering sexual orientation.

OUR GLORIOUS LESBIAN GOVERNOR?

In 2002, Linda Lingle shook up island politics by becoming the first Republican governor the 50th State had had since 1962. She was also the first female elected governor in Hawaii, the first Jewish governor in Hawaii, the first twice-divorced governor of Hawaii, and the first governor to not have any children. She is currently single.

Those later personal details are what have raised some eyebrows in Hawaii, not to mention Lingle's, shall we say, manly features. She does not have pierced ears—but she does don a bright trademark red lipstick. Either she's simply been picking up fashion tips from the lipstick lesbians on *The L-Word*, or the lady doth protest too much.

Lesbian rumors swirled around Lingle during her first gubernatorial race in 1998, when she was asked point blank if she was gay, a charge that was denied. A controversy ensued when Lingle supporters accused Democrats of spreading the rumor as a smear tactic—accusations that later proved untrue. To counter the disinformation campaign, Lingle even included a "Truth Box" section on her Web page to answer the rumors. Lingle's support of LGBT issues is mixed. She is definitely loads more liberal than her Republican counterparts on the Mainland when it comes to human rights issues, and she signed a bill in 2005 that prohibited landlords from discriminating against gay, lesbian, bisexual, and transgender people. But in 2005 she also vetoed another bill that would have added protections for gender identity to Hawaii's employment antidiscrimination law, violating one of her campaign promises. The veto prompted demonstrations by members of Kulia Na Mamo, a transgender support group. The state legislature did not override the veto.

So unfairly accused, or self-loathing lesbian? Only history will answer the rumors.

SOVEREIGNTY (ONIPAA)

History has not been kind to the Hawaiians. Their culture has been subverted, their population decimated, their land taken, their monarchy overthrown, and their language nearly lost. Through years of foreign diseases and intermarrying with immigrant races, there are less than a few thousand full-blooded Hawaiians left. Most live on the privately-owned island of Niihau. Not unlike Native Americans, Hawaiians have become strangers in their own land. However, unlike American Indians, Hawaiians do not have the legal rights to ancestral lands, economic autonomy, college tuition funds, and most importantly, they have no right to organize their own nation like Native Americans do.

This has helped fuel the islands' sovereignty movement, which is now focused on compensation for ceded lands. Most residents of Hawaii favor a "nation-within-a-nation" framework for the Hawaiian people. Most sovereignty activist groups seek only to have a council of native Hawaiians consulted to approve all land transactions in the state. The state has tried to hijack the sovereignty movement with bills influenced by financial institutions, which only make it harder for poor Hawaiians to make mortgage payments on homestead land. A handful of sovereignty groups advocate real secession from the United States, causing much controversy within the *haole* community.

The Hawaiian Sovereignty Movement largely overlaps with the Aloha Aina (literally: "love of the land") Movement, which started in the 1970s during the Hawaiian Cultural Renaissance, and it advocates the demilitarization of the islands by the U.S., indigenous recognition, cultural site protection, and ecological concerns that tie into the concept of *mlama ina,* or traditional land healing and restoration). The 1970s also saw intense land struggles such as that of Kalama Valley, Kahoolawe Island, and Waihole/Waikne, oftentimes with illegal occupation of these areas by native Hawaiians, actions that tied into sovereignty land rights issues.

Hawaii was put on the U.N. list in 1946 as a territory under U.S. control but was removed in 1959 when it became an American state. But a 1999 U.N. report advocated that Hawaii be returned to the U.N. list, due to the fact that the Hawaiian people never did officially and voluntarily relinquish their claim to sovereignty. The report claimed the plebiscite vote that led to Hawaii's statehood was in violation of article 73 of the United Nations charter.

In 1993, President Bill Clinton signed an official apology on behalf of the American businessmen who overthrew Queen Liliuokalani, the last sovereign Hawaiian monarch, in 1893. The apology acknowledged the deprivation of the rights of Native Hawaiians to self-determination, and referred to a 1988 study by the United States Justice Department, which concluded Congress did not have the authority to annex Hawaii by joint resolution.

On July 5, 2001, the Agent for the Hawaiian Kingdom, H.E. David Keanu Sai, Acting Minister of Interior, filed with the Security Council at United Nations headquarters in New York a Complaint against the United States of America concerning the prolonged occupation of the Hawaiian Islands since the Spanish-American War of 1898. The Complaint was filed with the Security Council in accordance with Article 35(2) of the United Nations Charter, which provides, "a State which is not a Member of the United Nations may bring to the attention of the Security Council or of the General Assembly any dispute to which it is a party if it accepts in advance, for the purpose of the dispute, the obligations of pacific settlement provided in the present Charter."

The Native Hawaiian Government Reorganization Act of 2007, a bill currently before the U.S. Congress, is commonly known as the Akaka Bill after U.S. Senator Daniel Akaka, who proposed various forms of this bill since 2000. The Akaka Bill seeks to establish a process for Native Hawaiians to gain federal recognition similar to the recognition that some Native American tribes currently possess.

Oddly enough, the bill is supported by Hawaii's Republican

Governor Linda Lingle, who said in 2003, "This is a historical issue, based on a relationship between an independent government and the United States of America, and what has happened since and the steps that we need to take to make things right."

The sovereignty movement is growing, and is a potentially divisive issue in the islands in the coming decades.

LGBT HAWAIIAN ACTIVISTS

Ku'umeaaloha Gomes is a professor at the University of Hawaii at Manoa, where she teaches a class on gays and lesbians in Hawaii. She is also the founder of Na Mamo O Hawaii (Hawaiian Lesbian and Gay Activists). She regularly holds anti-oppression workshops on interrupting oppressive behaviors. Although a big part of her work is about the sovereignty issue for native Hawaiians, Gomes explains her group is multi-issue. "We wanted to show that the same-sex marriage issue is not just about middle-class, white transplants to the islands, but also about people that are born here, in our family."

The issue of heterosexism is also a factor for Hawaiians as well. "We as native Hawaiians who are gay do not want our Hawaiian community to become our colonizers, and prevent us from our equality in society…Na Mamo O Hawaii is trying to be the bridge between the Hawaiian and the gay communities. That's what makes me so tired!"

Gomes' view is that heterosexism, sexism, racism, and classism are all inter-related, and must be tackled as a whole. "The gay communities and the Hawaiian movement need to interact. The native people are the most oppressed here, with no right to self-government, and the gay community cannot isolate the issues… For a lot of residents, they have come here as gay people into this place, and they have to realize that the native Hawaiians are their

AIDS IN HAWAII

With the frequently closeted aspect of island society, HIV/ AIDS has been an ongoing problem in Hawaii, especially for native Hawaiians. According to Ke Ola Mamo (the Native Hawaiian Health Care System), Hawaiians and part-Hawaiians are diagnosed with AIDS and HIV proportionally higher than any other Asian or Pacific Islander group in Hawaii. In fact, more than twice the rate of the next highest Asian/Pacific Islander group, the Chinese. From 1986–1995, the number of Hawaiians with AIDS jumped up 157%, compared with 99% for the state's population as a whole. Prevention efforts have focused on innovative education with Hawaiian values in mind, and better access to health care for Hawaiians, who have one of the lowest health profiles in the nation.

From 1983 to 2005, AIDS claimed 1,708 lives in Hawaii, although unofficial statistics are probably much higher. Up to 172 people died from the disease in the mid-90s, but now the number has stabilized at around 40 deaths per year. Of interest, the *State of Hawaii Data Handbook* recorded Hawaii's first AIDS causality was not a gay man, but an Asian woman 50 years of age. And it took place over a quarter of a century ago! The unnamed woman was diagnosed with a mysterious illness in May of 1978, and succumbed in August of that same year. It was later discovered she had AIDS.

hosts. You should know the history, understand it, and celebrate the culture."

Most important, Ku'umeaaloha stresses people to ask, "If I'm going to participate in this, what am I going to give back to the Hawaiians? These people are sharing their culture with me: do I stand up for them, or stand back from it? What do I do to keep these people and their culture alive?"

UNDERSTANDING HAWAIIAN CULTURE FOR THE OUT TRAVELER

HOW IS HOMO HAWAII?

Hawaii. Just the word conjures up mystic waterfalls and hula dancers and sunshine and ocean and, well, lots of queer boys and girls trying to experience a Fantasy Island of tolerant peoples, liberal politics, and most importantly, thong bikini weather. As with most fantasy lands, the reality is tons more interesting and varied. Hawaii at the beginning of the twenty-first century is a land of mass tourism, high costs of living, cultural conflicts, racial pressures, and economic uncertainty.

Now the good news: It is still an absolutely incredible place to encounter. The islands are filled with empty lava deserts, snow-capped volcanoes, huge valley systems, dripping rain forests, spectacular coral reefs, all thousands of miles from any continent. Hawaii will always hold her magic. And she hides her secrets well. The traveler will need much time and many return visits (not to mention an open heart) to truly get to know Hawaii.

The islands host some of the most amazing people you will ever be privileged to meet on the planet. Naturally warm, generous, and kind, island residents are rightfully proud of their spiritually significant heritage of "aloha." *Aloha* is a word that does not merely mean hello and good-bye, but *love*. To live *aloha* simply means to live in the light, to do unto others as you would have them do unto you, to actively pursue love every day. *Aloha* is the keystone of understanding Hawaiian culture. It's the mystical attribute that draws people back to her shores again and again in search of its profound meaning.

THE CONCEPT OF THE *OHANA*

Geographically limited and forced to rely on one another to survive, Hawaiians have always emphasized harmony and acceptance of individual differences. Everyone has a place in society. An *ohana* means relatives and friends who make up an extended "village" of people who know and look after each other. After all, everyone in old Hawaii (and modern Hawaii for that matter) were related in one way or another, and had to get along with one another and work together on specks of land surrounded by a huge ocean. Thus, Hawaiian culture has always been traditionally tolerant with its renowned "hang loose" attitude. Subsequent immigrant groups for the most part have embraced this attitude, making for a society where unique distinctions are celebrated and seen as beneficial.

The concept of *ohana* generally includes gays and lesbians too. This is, after all, a culture where men are encouraged to wear flowers on their head and sing falsetto. With the 1997 Reciprocal Beneficiaries Act, legally gays have more partnership rights than in many other parts of the U.S.—and there is hope that one of the three same-sex marriage bills currently in the state legislature will soon become law. Many straights will pop up in gay restaurants or gay bars without a hint of embarrassment. In fact, almost all gay businesses around the state cater to both straights and queers.

Mainland homos have been moving to the islands for decades, including a large wave in the '70s. Some are turned on by the warm culture and climate; others come for reasons of health, or simply to escape the Mainland energy. A lot find that residing in the islands, with its high cost of living and limited opportunities, is a much different experience than vacationing on the islands, and a portion move back after a short stint. Modern Hawaii can be a transient society where Mainlanders and immigrants come and go, and sometimes it takes years to become fully integrated into a community's *ohana*. Locals will often ask how long you have lived in the islands before making a concerted effort to begin a friendship. They want to know *malihini* (island newcomers) are here for the long haul before they invest a lot of time in relationships, since once you have an island friend you will usually have them for life.

The Mainland gays who stay, bring with them a more "out" sense of identity, and have invigorated and organized the island's overall queer community, although "white-washing" it in the process. Separated from their own Mainland families for one reason or another, these *haoles* and other Mainlanders are more involved with politics and setting up an alternative gay society. The locally born and raised don't feel the need to be as strident in their gayness. Their focus is more on the *ohana* and their own extended community.

OUT LIKE *MAHU* OR OUT LIKE GAY?

Some visitors expect Hawaii to be a homo holiday party heaven like Palm Springs, Provincetown, or Key West. Well, wrong! Hawaii's first real circuit party, Honolulu's Volcano Party, only began in 2002. Hawaii is actually more for the eco-adventure or honeymooning types. Many travelers with high expectations of a large and out gay scene in Hawaii are usually disappointed. Despite the attention Hawaii gets for its liberal politics and lifestyle, there are no real gayboorhoods, no all-gay resort areas, and relatively few gay or lesbian island establishments to patronize. And as with a lot of small

THE YEAR OF THE *MAHU*

Two thousand one was a big year for the *mahu*. Andrew Matzner published the introspective book entitled, *O Au No Kiea*, translated as "This Is Me," and the documentary film *Ke Kulana He Mahu* was directed by Kathryn Xian and Brent Anbe. The award-winning film, which showed in international film festivals, interviewed history scholars and oral traditionalists about the role of the *mahu* and current-day island politics.

The book *O Au No Kiea* was the first work of its kind, with in-depth interviews of over a dozen Oahu *mahu*, many former prostitutes, delving deep into the causes of what led these people into prostitution (since *mahu* sometimes get kicked out of their families' homes). Matzner hopes the insightful book will someday be read in Hawaii schools, and used "as a tool to convey to a wide audience the humanity of a group of people for whom it is so often denied."

businesses in Hawaii, many gay-oriented ones have a hard time surviving. The reasons could be isolation, island culture, and lack of community support. Ironically, it's probably also due to the fact that gays are more integrated into the general society here than in other places.

Still, the actual attitude toward out gays and lesbians is and always has been a mixed bag. The reality is varied, especially from island to island. It is safe to say a majority of residents don't really care if you're gay. But on the other hand, Hawaii still has a strong family-based society with Asian influences, and one that has increasingly become more religious and conservative over the last couple of decades. For many local gays and lesbians it's a "don't ask, don't tell" policy as far as being out, publicly or privately.

Coming out on an island where everyone has known you since you were a kid may not even be necessary in the Mainland sense. You just are who you are, no explanation or gory details necessary, since forwardness has always been frowned upon in the Hawaiian culture. Many local gays and lesbians don't identify themselves with the mainstream gay world at all. Their race or heritage is a much more important trait than their mere sexual orientation.

This leads to a situation where many island residents never bother coming out at all. There are many stories of local men who enjoy having sex with gay men, only to remain in a heterosexual posture, never admitting to, or fully living out, their true tendency. It's common for these closeted men to remain living with their families, all the while pursuing guys on the side. Since they are not "muffy" (effeminate) types, they are not "gay." Of course this is a generalization, but you hear tales of even straight police officers keeping male *mahu* lovers on the side for years.

On the Mainland, it seems "straight-acting" gay men are somehow more accepted within the cultural framework, while effeminate men can be ridiculed or are more of a threat to the hyper-macho society. In Hawaii, the opposite probably holds true. Effeminate men are historically accepted within the Polynesian culture, and one finds many "muffies" (aka *mahu* in Hawaii) happily integrated in Samoa, Tahiti, and other parts of the Pacific. *Mahu* are revered for their talents in the arts (particularly *hula*) and are usually not rejected by their families.

The story is different from island to island and ethnic group to ethnic group. A common saying is "Everyone's a minority in Hawaii." Most people born on the islands are of mixed Asian, Pacific

DO GAY GUYS SURF?

Surfing is one the great gifts Hawaii has given to the rest of the world. The first European visitors drew pictures of naked young men riding the waves on long pieces of wood, and ever since, Oahu has been one of the major surf capitals of the world.

Like other testosterone sports, gay men love the image of the wet and rippled surfer coming out of the waves with his shiny board. But the surf world is notorious for being macho, homophobic, and wary of outsiders. But that changed in Hawaii in 1999 when Doug Smith ran a small ad in the back of the *Honolulu Weekly* stating a gay surf club was forming. Sheepish e-mails from closeted surfers began to trickle in, and then out gay men who never ventured to try the sport felt braver to do so, and now the gay surf club meets in front of the open arms of the Duke Kahanamoku statue (an Olympic swimmer and the most famous surfer who ever lived) in Waikiki weekly, with over two dozen participants on any given Saturday. One of the few gay surf groups in the world, the group has inspired others to form similar clubs on the West Coast of the U.S.

"I had been surfing since I was six in California, after my father learned how to surf in Hawaii and taught me and my brothers," explains Doug. "When I came back to live in Hawaii after having gone to school here, I knew I wanted to make surfing part of my life, because it's easy to get busy and miss the reason why you even live here."

DO GAY GUYS SURF?

After spending a lot of time hanging out with straight surfers and hiding his sexuality, Doug thought it would be nice to surf with someone he could be himself around. He was sure there were other closeted surfers, but he knew they would be hard to find. But after the ad ran, "One of the first people who contacted me was a local boy who had been in surfing contests while growing up here. He was adorable, and a closet case, but he surfed with us. He thought that it was great, but he was not into exposing his sexuality, like a typical local surfer boy. At least I think we helped him come out a bit." Doug says that most of the other surfers in the group have lived on Oahu for years and always wanted to learn the sport, but never had the guts to do it. "The fact that we give free lessons I think helps people step up to the plate."

And what is the typical Saturday crowd? "We get some guys in the military that are closeted, and there's a local lesbian couple who joins us a lot. We get a lot of people who hear about us through the grapevine and visitors show up from as far away as New Zealand, Spain, Ireland, Australia, and Brazil. We even had a whole family from Holland once who absolutely loved it!" Besides the Saturday group, the core surfers have begun to explore other surf spots on the North Shore and around the island of Oahu.

"They keep asking us to be in the Gay Pride parade, but we haven't done it yet," Doug admits in typically shy surfer fashion. "But surfing is so much a part of our culture here.

UNDERSTANDING HAWAIIAN CULTURE FOR THE OUT TRAVELER

DO GAY GUYS SURF?

A lot of people leave saying they surfed in Hawaii, and they remember it for the rest of their lives. It's a huge deal to them."

To find out more about the group or to join them on Saturdays, surf (the net) to GROUPS.YAHOO.COM/GROUP/ GAYSURFCLUBHAWAII or call (808) 779-7934.

Islander, and/or European descent. Sadly, pure-blooded Hawaiians are few and far between, although there are a lot of people that are part-Hawaiian. Most non-white people get lumped into the category of "locals." However, locals may still be proud of their Filipino, Samoan, or Japanese roots and practices. Thus, Hawaii calls itself a "mixed plate." A minority's distinct attitude toward gays can override the general consensus.

EVERY ISLE TELLS A DIFFERENT QUEER STORY

Within the islands, gay lifestyles can vary radically. Being gay on Oahu, with its openly homo beaches and bars, means a completely different thing than on rural Molokai, where wearing full-time cross-dressing is an acceptable way to be "queer." Honolulu presents more of a metropolitan gay singles scene. Many gays born and raised in Hawaii turn toward Honolulu, with its anonymity, as "the mainland." On islands outside of Oahu, you will tend to find gays and lesbians coupled up or living with families. There is only one bona fide gay bar beyond Oahu, and Honolulu is the only place that holds a gay pride parade. The neighbor islands tend to have smaller, closer-knit societies where meeting other gays can prove difficult—

save for a handful of beaches and cruising spots. Many island-born gays take off to the continents and larger cities to experience a more anonymous Mainland gay lifestyle—notably they tend toward Los Angeles, Las Vegas, and the San Francisco Bay Area.

LGBT communities between the islands don't interact much, except maybe through Honolulu. They usually have no clue what the others are even doing! Some visitors know much more about gay Hawaii than gay residents do. This geographical isolation makes for a distinct mood on each neighbor island. It has been said that the Hawaiian Islands are like sisters, each with their own personality and character, which is mirrored in each isle's gay communities.

Gays in Hawaii still face the same challenges as anywhere. In some island neighborhoods, towns, and beaches, gay or lesbian couples may not feel terribly welcome at all. Public displays of affection do not happen too often between gays, even in Honolulu. Gay bashing is not unheard of, job and housing discrimination happens, and undercover stings on cruise spots, with televising of the offender's face as a shame tactic, have also occurred. Although many local Christian churches accept openly gay members, there are those who don't fully understand or appreciate Jesus' example and teachings, and attack the gays they should love.

The question is: Do queers overall have it better here than elsewhere? The answer is a conditional yes. Depends on who you ask. Without a doubt, Hawaii will continue to be at the forefront of the new gay and lesbian dawning, showing the entire world what love and acceptance and aloha really mean.

HAWAIIAN MYTHOLOGY

The Hawaiian myths are colored by larger-than-life figures who earn fear and respect, and belief in them is still very much alive today, despite the onslaught of missionary teaching and American

THE RAINBOW

If you are from the Mainland, you may think Hawaii is more gay-friendly than you ever dreamed when you spot all the usages of the rainbow symbol around the state. Tons of business names have the word in their titles ("Rainbow Books," "Rainbow Vacuum Cleaners"). The colors are splashed on many buildings, and the spectrum shows up on the state's automobile license plates and driver's licenses. The University of Hawaii's famous men's volleyball team (the nation's top) were called "The Rainbows" up until 2000 when finally they caught on to the homo connotation and changed their name to the butcher "Warriors." Even the state capital's official Web site once proudly announced, "Welcome to the Rainbow Connection!" before they evidently caught on too.

Sorry to burst your bubble, but as you probably figured out, the rainbow (*anuenue* in Hawaiian) does not have the same homosexual connotation in Hawaii that it does in other places. In fact, the rainbow acts as an emblem for Hawaii itself, since they are always popping up all over the state year-round. Maybe that's why queers and the islands attract each other the way they do!

Rainbows in ancient Hawaii weren't always as gay. Rainbows could mean a sign of death, or bad luck during a journey. On the flip side, they could mean the presence of high chiefs, and during childbirth, the rainbow foretold of a blessed child.

media influences. Many are the island stories of spotting Pele hitchhiking, or a mischievous dwarf-like *menehune* ducking behind a tree. Interest in *huna*, or ancient Hawaiin magic and beliefs, is growing in modern times. What's more, islanders believe in the innate spirituality of the land itself—you'll often hear people in Hawaii talking about the *mana* (spirit) or the *aina* (land). This feeling of metaphysical connection to the land is so strong that many island-born (and tourists, for that matter) feel the need to return time and time again to recharge their spiritual batteries with the intense power of the islands themselves. Understanding Hawaiian mythology and spirituality is an important part of understanding Hawaii as a whole.

Hawaiian myths can be varied and at times seem to contradict one another (depending on the source), but are overall consistent with the surprisingly uniform mythology of all the far-flung bits of land that make up Polynesia. The four main deities in the Hawaiian pantheon are Ku (the god of war), Kanaloa (the god of the ocean), Kane (the god of light and the sky), and Lono (the god of fertility and peace). All four existed before time began, and each has other associations—for instance, Kanaloa is sometimes characterized also as the god of the underworld. Kane (a word you'll see on bathroom doors since it also means "man") and Kanaloa are yin-yang figures, since the former is associated with South, the latter with North. Since the two are closely linked in many chants, it's led some gays to claim them as "family," but this probably isn't the case since certain legends state that Kane was married to Na Wahine (*wahine* being another frequently-seen word that means "woman").

Like in ancient Greece or Rome, there are scores of other interrelated gods and goddesses who work up all kinds of dramas in numerous myths, but two especially stand out in modern-day Hawaii: Pele and Maui.

HELL HATH NO FURY LIKE THE GODDESS PELE

Pele, the goddess of volcanoes and fire, is one of the most honored and revered figures in Hawaiian culture. And the most famous. She's tough, ornery, temperamental, and always in a fight with someone—although she also has a creative, nurturing side to her as well. It was Pele who loaded up a bunch of her deity brothers and headed north from Tahiti in a canoe, in order to rid herself of her troublesome sister, the goddess of the sea Namakaokahai. The group set foot on Niihau Island first. As soon as Pele started digging her volcanic holes, her sister would promptly put them out with waves of seawater.

Frustrated, Pele moved on to dig up Kauai, then Oahu, then Maui, and finally ended up on the island of Hawaii, all the time thwarted by her meddling sister who destroyed every volcano Pele attempted to prolong. As with every great legend, there's a ring of truth: Niihau is indeed the oldest of the main Hawaiian Islands, formed by a volcanic hot spot in the earth's crust, and every island was geologically formed in the order in which Pele was said to have inhabited them.

Some legends state that Namakaokahai finally killed Pele, but as always, Pele had the last laugh. Her spirit dug a hole far from the shoreline and her sister's sea water, and thus the spectacular crater of Kilauea was formed. Halemaumau Crater at the Hawaii Volcanoes National Park is still the sacred home of Pele, and park visitors may spot flowers and gin bottles (purportedly Pele's favorite drink) left as offerings there. Belief in Pele is as strong among islanders as it is with the tourists who won't dare take lava rocks off the island for fear of Pele's retribution (even though the national park is sometimes credited for having started that one).

If you see a glorious young woman with long black hair walking alongside an island road, or perhaps an old woman with a white dog, be sure to look twice. There are many accounts of people giving the woman a ride, when she suddenly disappears. Lesbians in particular love Pele's goddess powers, and it's no wonder the Big Island, and in particular the district of Puna adjoining the national park, has a large lesbian population.

MAUI: HALF MAN, HALF GOD

Maui is named after a Herculean figure in Hawaiian mythology: a half man, half god who possessed great *mana* or spiritual power. His legend is known throughout Polynesia. Even in far away New Zealand stories about Maui abound. His traditional home is the Haleakala Crater on Maui, the largest dormant volcano in the world. Most legends say it was the heroic Maui who pulled up the very islands of Hawaii from the depths of the ocean with his magic fishhook (which is now a Polynesian star constellation in Scorpius). It was also he who lassoed the sun with fiber ropes in order to slow down its procession across the sky, so the working day would be longer (and seems to be getting longer by the minute!). A cunning trickster, Maui stole the knowledge of fire-making from the mud hens of Oahu, and gave the knowledge to humans. Maui is also credited for using his strength to raise the sky up to its current position.

Obviously not one to shy away from a challenge, there's a tale of Maui attempting to conquer death itself. A New Zealand myth tells of a nude and muscled Maui, spear in hand, jumping into the mouth of Hinenuitepo, the goddess of death, in order to rip out her heart and thus bring immortality to the world. Unfortunately, she awoke and bit Maui in two as he tried to escape and thus came the dramatic, operatic finale of Maui, Hawaii's Superman.

KAUAI'S MENEHUNE

The *menehune* are Hawaii's race of legendary little people who live in the islands' mountains and caves. The little buggers are credited with creating marvelous engineering feats throughout Hawaii, like irrigation ditches, fish ponds, and temples, which are especially prevalent on Kauai. The banana-loving *menehune* build quickly and swiftly, often in one night, possess magical powers, and are super cute to boot. (If you don't spot one on your own, pick up the popular local bottled water brand *Menehune* to view their likeness). Archaeologists agree that the intricate style of construction of *menehune* works, as well as their distinct markings, bear no resemblance to works done by ancient Hawaiians. A more boring explanation is that the name *menehune* was given to the first migration of Tahitians to the islands by subsequent arrivals from the south. *Manahune* means "outcast" in Tahitian, and elsewhere in old South Pacific it referred to a servant class of laborers. Fairies or construction workers? We'll let you decide…

HAWAIIAN MUSIC AND DANCE

A newfound interest in island culture and identity took off in the 1970s and is now called the Hawaiian Renaissance. Music and dance were at the forefront of the popular movement, and continue to be catalysts for younger generations to get in touch with their culture and language.

THE IMPORTANCE OF HULA

Hula itself has been called the lifeblood of the Hawaiian people, and stands as one of the most truly original dance forms in the world.

Hula along with *mele* (chants) were the main form of storytelling and handing down of information for the ancient Hawaiians, in place of a written language. Not only were legends and tales told through hula, but also important historical events and royal lineage. For years, students would train under a *kumu hula*, who would scrutinize with an eagle eye to make sure not one movement was off, which might alter the meaning of a dance. Although hula is known for its swaying hips, the dancers' hands, arms, feet, face, and general movement all convey meaning.

Interestingly, some scholars say men were the only ones allowed to dance hula in the very old days. They were the only ones allowed at *heiau* (temples) to perform the religious dance, although it's speculated women had their own *heiau* and hula as well. Muscular males would enact the precise dance clad only in *malo* (loincloths); grass skirts were introduced to hula only about a century ago via immigrants from the modern-day island nation of Kiribati to the south of Hawaii. Western missionaries suppressed what they saw as a lewd, suggestive dance, leading many, especially *mahu* (gay men), to keep the dance alive in secret..

King Kalakaua (known as the "Merrie Monarch" for his love of dance and parties) resurrected the hula as a cultural art form in the late 1800s. Women had to wear skirts and tops, while men could still don skimpy *malo*. The dance also resurfaced in the 1930s and '40s, thanks to popular radio and then TV shows that mixed orchestration and English songs with hula. This created the more modern version of *hapa haole* (half white) hula, the watered-down form most Americans conjure when they think of hula as pure camp.

Nowadays, hula falls into two categories. The *kahiko hula* (ancient) involved traditional instruments or dress, and is serious in tone. A *kumu hula* sits on the ground drumming a hollow gourd and chanting an old *mele*, with the dancers also involved call-and-response chanting. The *'auana hula* (modern) is much freer and more jovial in style, and can depict topics as contemporary as airplane travel, surf tournaments, even basketball games! *'Auana hula* usually includes a band of some sort.

In 1963, the Merrie Monarch Festival formed on the Big Island, acting as a venue for hula competition and appreciation. Today the festival is broadcast live across the state starting Easter Sunday and lasting a week. Many *halau* (hula troupes) compete from around the world. Ironically, only women performed at the festival until the men's division was introduced in 1976. Today, a majority of hula's great teachers and performers are gay and/or effeminate men, and their skill and love of the dance has helped to rejuvenate this truly Hawaiian art form.

THE IMPORTANCE OF MUSIC

Many outsiders with little exposure to Hawaiian music assume it is a cheesy brand of archaic, monotonous, or unrefined melodies that act merely as back-up for smiling hula girls. They may only think of it in terms of corniness, along with plastic grass skirts, toy ukuleles, or Don Ho. Nothing could be further from the truth. Hawaiian music is a varied, evolving, and rich art form that is central to the ongoing renaissance of the island chain's unique culture.

Hula and *mele* (chants) were of immense importance to a people without a written language, and the islands' emphasis on music as a cultural core is still strong today. Certain instruments evoke Hawaii in themselves: the ukulele (correctly pronounced *ook–oo–lay–lay*) translates as "jumping flea" due to the fast finger movements. It was originally derived from the braguinha, an instrument brought over by Portuguese laborers, and is supposed to be the easiest instrument in the world to learn.

The steel guitar, another staple of modern Hawaiian music, was invented in 1889 by native Hawaiian Joseph Kekuku. It is said that the steel guitar and banjo are the only two major instruments to have been invented in the U.S.A. The steel guitar is usually played with slack-key tuning, hence the name slack-key music. The light, melodic twangs of the strings sound uniquely Hawaiian. The late Gabby Pahinui, credited with bringing the instrument back into distinction in the '70s, is still probably the most famous slack-key guitarist in the world.

Like the islands themselves, contemporary Hawaiian music is a "mixed plate." Most performers have quite a range of styles, from love ballads sung in Hawaiian, to modern folk-rock numbers, to ancient chants. Men sing some or all of their songs in a high-pitched falsetto. Jamaican reggae is also popular in Hawaii, and a local hybrid version has emerged dubbed "Jawaiian."

As with hula and other island art forms, gays are prominent in the local music scene. The only out lesbian singer in Hawaii, Oahu resident Kim Char Meredith, released a popular lesbian-themed, country/pop CD titled *A Slender Line of Lavender* in 1998 (she had previously recorded four contemporary Christian albums), as well as *Give and Take* in 2003. Says Kim, "My music is my therapy to process emotions—to focus on the essence of what I really feel. The record companies don't want me to narrow my niche and become a lesbian singer, but I have a very strong women's following, and I'm proud of it."

One of Hawaii's biggest-selling artists to date, Maui resident Kealii Reichel, climbed *Billboard's* world music charts with his albums *Kawaipunahele* and *Lei Halia*. His album *E O Mai* included a song about the AIDS quilt. Says Kealii, "Not everyone will like our music, but my job is to educate as well as to entertain...to

CAMP HAWAII-WOOD

With fake grass skirts, scantily clad "natives," "primitive" locales, and warbly "island" tunes, Hawaii has been fertile ground for campy movie making on the grandest of scales. Hollywood has always had a way of gloriously distorting fact and fiction, and its flashy and trashy exploitation of the South Seas is no exception. Little thought or respect has been given to the Polynesian history, culture, or damage by Western influences—Hooray for Hollywood! The exceptions are great historical films like *Hawaii*, *Mutiny on the Bounty*, and more recently, *Rapa Nui* starring Hawaii's own beefcake, Jason Scott Lee. Au contraire, Hawaii and other tropical isles have merely served as an exotic Hollywood backdrop for the adventures of white people. And what a tawdry ride it's been:

***BIRD OF PARADISE* (1932)** Windward Oahu impersonates "the island of Lani" in this story of a white man who runs off with an island princess. She, of course, ends up sacrificing herself into a flaming volcano at the end, something never practiced in Polynesia. In this pre-code classic, Dolores Del Rio does a topless "native" dance with a flower lei taped carefully across her chest.

***FOUR FRIGHTENED PEOPLE* (1934)** Claudette Colbert's virginal makeup is barely smudged in this malarkey Cecil B. De Mille tale of four Caucasians shipwrecked in Malaysia and forced to fend for themselves in a jungle full of scary natives,

CAMP HAWAII-WOOD

cobras, and ruins of past civilizations. It was shot around Hilo on the Big Island, although the movie proudly declares in the opening credits it was filmed in the South Pacific—did the studio not own a world map?

MISS SADIE THOMPSON (1953) The famous W. Somerset Maugham tale of a sordid Honolulu "entertainer" on her way to redemption in Pago Pago is given the 3-D musical Technicolor treatment, in this garish version starring Rita Hayworth. Shot mainly around the Coco Palms Resort on Kauai.

THE REVOLT OF MAMIE STOVER (1956) Based on actual pre–WWII Honolulu red-light characters, the perpetually buxom Jane Russell plays the titular role in this story of an ambitious Waikiki dance hall girl who becomes the "Henry Ford of harlotry," and amasses her fortune in island real estate.

NAKED PARADISE (1957) Exploitation king Roger Corman's entry into the South Seas genre, this convoluted story about crooks using a charter boat to rob a pineapple plantation barely lives up to the film's promise of "Temptation and terror in a savage land of wild desire!"

SHE GODS OF SHARK REEF (1958) Another one of Corman's glorious B pictures, the plot, if you can call it that,

CAMP HAWAII-WOOD

is about two shipwrecked survivors washed up on an isolated island inhabited only by women. Shot back-to-back in Kauai with *Naked Paradise*.

BLUE HAWAII (1961) This was the first and best known of the handful of Hawaiian-made features for Elvis. Here he's the son of a pineapple plantation owner who becomes a tour guide for pretty girls in tight outfits, crooning the title tune actually made popular by Bing Crosby.

GIDGET GOES HAWAIIAN (1961) This was the first sequel to 1959's *Gidget*, with a plot revolving around whether or not our heroine will give up her virginity to Moondoggie on Waikiki beach (I'll let you guess the outcome).

DIAMOND HEAD (1963) One of the rare Hawaii films to deal with racism, Charlton Heston camps it up (more than usual) as the pig-headed, bullwhip-wielding owner of a pineapple plantation (what's up with pineapples and Hollywood?), who freaks when his sister marries a full-blooded Hawaiian.

GOIN' COCONUTS (1978) A vehicle for big-toothed Donny and Marie Osmond, who are chased around the islands by crooks trying to swipe Marie's necklace. No surprise the siblings get to yodel their way through this one!

CAMP HAWAII-WOOD

WHEN TIME RAN OUT (1980) In this, the cheesiest volcano flick of all time (and that's saying something), Paul Newman and Jacqueline Bisset stay at a posh resort (now the Sheraton Keauhou on the Big Island) threatened by the worst papier-mâché volcano and blue-screen tidal waves you have ever laid eyes on. Solely for film masochists.

BLACK WIDOW (1986) This film noir about a sexually ambiguous federal agent (Debra Winger) tracking a beautiful killer (Teresa Russell) to Hawaii, has enough overt lesbian "subtext" to make it look like a sequel to *Personal Best*. Locations include the actual eruption site of Kilauea on the Big Island, spewing lava up 1,000 feet.

JOE VERSUS THE VOLCANO (1990) A movie Tom Hanks would like to wipe off the face of cinematic history, this one includes every South Seas cliché on record: bizarre native rituals, natural disaster, and human sacrifice into a volcano (Pele never went for that in real Hawaii!). Shot on Oahu's North Shore—where there are active volcanoes.

EXIT TO EDEN (1994) Film critic Leonard Maltin perfectly summed up this asinine comedy (based on an Anne Rice novel!) a "strange cinematic catastrophe." It stars our fave Rosie O'Donnell and Dan Akroyd as undercover cops on an S&M fantasy island ruled by a flustered dominitrix. Filmed at Lanai's otherwise tasteful Manele Bay Resort.

CAMP HAWAII-WOOD

BLUE CRUSH (2002) What's more important to surfing? That seems to be the central theme in this bikini flick starring Kate Bosworth, who whines her way through the dilemma of whether she can date an NFL player and compete in the Pipe Masters on Oahu's North Shore simultaneously. A saccharin, bubble-gum soundtrack is added for drama.

make people think about who we are as Hawaiians. We don't run around naked, we don't live in grass shacks. We are modern. We are educated. We are a living, viable, important culture with a voice."

Other gay island recording artists include The Brothers Cazimero, a duo (one gay, one straight) that has been popular on the island scene for years, and most of their work includes a traditional Hawaiian flavor. Hometown favorite and out performer Matt Yee dons some fabulous dresses for his fun piano lounge act at Honolulu nightspots and on gay Hawaii cruises. Nathan Kalama on Kauai founded the Mokihana Festival and has also produced a CD of Hawaiian favorites.

Other mainstream island singers worth catching for their unique and individual sounds are Sistah Robi Kahakalau, the female trio Na Leo Pilimehana, the late Israel Kamakawiwoole, the Peter Moon Band, and many others. And don't forget gay icon Bette Midler was also raised on Oahu. The Hawaiian music industry continues to take off, so keep watching those charts!

LEARNING THE LINGO

Sadly, Hawaiian as a proper language became mostly lost during the twentieth century. Younger generations lost touch with the ancient island tongue in English-dominated society, making for relatively few residents who now speak fluent Hawaiian. The language was banned outright after the Hawaiian monarchy's overthrow by American businessmen in the 1890s. It has only recently made a comeback in the state as a whole, with popular Hawaiian language preschools for children, radio shows, Web sites, and classes. The privately-owned, purely Hawaiian island of Niihau is the last outpost in the world where Hawaiian is spoken as a first language, and English as a second.

Hawaiian is very similar to other Polynesian languages, despite the presence of other letters in languages like Tahitian and Maori. When Captain Cook, the first European believed to have discovered Hawaii, first met the locals here, he spoke Tahitian which was generally understood by the Hawaiians of the time.

PRONUNCIATION NOTES

The Hawaiian language has the shortest alphabet in the world with a mere 12 letters: the vowels A, E, I, O, U (with Latin pronunciation like vowels in Spanish or French) and the consonants H, K, L, M, N, P and W.

The long vowel macron (-), called a *kahak* in Hawaiian, stresses a vowel and denotes to hold the sound longer. The presence of an *okina* and/or a *kahak* can alter the meaning of a word, and both are coming back into general usage—you often see them on signs in Hawaii.

With or without marks, Hawaiian can be daunting to try to pronounce for the uninitiated. Vowels tend to be clumped together, and some are technically pronounced differently on different syllables. Many vowels are slurred together in general speech anyway.

CONSONANTS

P and k are pronounced about the same as in English but with less aspiration.

H, l, m, n are pronounced about the same as in English.

W—after i and e, sounds like a v; after u and o, it sounds like w; after an a it is either w or v.

VOWELS, UNSTRESSED

A like *a* in above
E like *e* in set
I like *y* in city
O like *o* in mole
U like *oo* in soon

VOWELS, STRESSED

A, like *a* in above
E like *e* in set
E like *ay* in play
I, like *ee* in fee
I, like *o* in mole
U, like *oo* in soon

HAWAIIAN

Hawaiian words will still creep up in local conversation and signage and place names. Here are some commonly-used ones you'll frequently come across:

aloha – spirit of love and kindness, also hello and good-bye

ina – land

alii – Hawaiian royalty

akamai – clever, smart

hale – house

hana – work

haole – Caucasian

heiau – Hawaiian temple

ipo – sweetheart

kahuna – priest or expert teacher

kai – ocean, sea

kamaina – island resident

kne – male

kapu – forbidden, taboo

keiki – baby or child

kkua – help

kona – leeward side of an island

kupuna – elder

lnai – verandah or porch

lomilomi – traditional Hawaiian massage

lua – toilet

mahalo – thank you

mh – transvestite, or gay man in general

makai – toward the ocean

malihini – island newcomer

mana – spiritual power

mauka – toward the mountains

ohana – family, close friends

okele – buttocks

ono – tasty

pali – cliffs

paniolo – island cowboy
pau – finish, end
puka – hole
pp – appetizers
wahine – woman
wikiwiki – quickly, in a rush

PIDGIN

In Hawaii, you will also hear lots of Pidgin, which is technically called Hawaii Creole English. Pidgin (a bastardized word for "business") has its roots in old plantation days where different nationalities and ethnicities needed to communicate with the white landowners and with each other. But it's not a language so much as idiosyncratic local phrases and slang with a distinct island accent. It has evolved a long way over the years and picked up much street credibility. Pidgin is predominantly used by native "locals" and some long-time *haoles*.

Proper Hawaiian and the informal Pidgin are often used together. Pidgin is colorful, fun, and usually hard to understand to the uninitiated. *Ass wy dem touriss buggahs 'ave such a har time, yeah?* The worst is hearing a visitor clumsily attempt to say something in Pidgin or use a local accent, to the embarrassment of everyone involved! (Be sure to read the following DON'T section.) So use these words as reference only:

ass wy – that's why
beef – fight
brah – good friend (short for brother)
broke da mouth – unbelievably delicious
buggah – difficult thing or person
bummahs – bummer, too bad

choice – great
choke – a lot of
da – the (as in "da store")
fo' real – really
grinds – food
howzit – How's it going?
junk – lousy
kau kau – food, chow
lakas – loins
latahs – see you later
lesgo – let's go
manini – small-time, stingy
mek ass – make a fool of yourself
one – used in place of "a" or "an"
pupule – crazy, insane
talk story – converse, chat
tita – a rugged gal
try wait – please hold on
tutu – auntie, wise old woman
stink eye – dirty look
shi-shi – pee-pee
suck um up – drink, as in beer
whatevahz – whatever

And the honorary degree goes to: Da kine— loosely translated to English as "whatchamacallit." Da kine is the cornerstone of Pidgin. Without it, life would not function as known in Hawaii. You'll want to use da kine when you're in one da kine bar and one da kine comes up to you and starts looking all da kine and you wonder if you should go to the da kine, but then you think da kine…

MIND YOUR ISLAND MANNERS

Now, one thing most people agree on is that Hawaii is not part of the U.S. Don't tell me about the Fiftieth State and all that: Hawaii is a separate, unique culture, apart from North America. And you, as the inane visitor that you are, are bound to violate at least several social codes here, shaming your family for generations! Fortunately the local populace is aware of your impending touristy blunders (as they have seen them all before), and you have their aloha on your side.

DON'T:

FAKE A LOCAL ACCENT or talk Pidgin in an attempt to woo the island residents. This has got to be the lamest thing visitors try, and you end up looking like a fool (that's if you aren't one already).

LEAVE YOUR SHOES ON IN THE HOUSE or any personal human dwelling for that matter. You have now tracked in all kinds of dirt that Auntie must get down on her knees to scrub out, you Mainland fool! We don't care how bad your feet stink from all those stupid thick socks, boots, and/or heels you wear over there. No shame, okay brah?

GO TO SOMEONE'S HOUSE EMPTY HANDED. Oh boy, if someone showed up at my door after I invited 'em over for grinds, and not even bring me one beer or one flower or notin', I would think that's one stingy *buggah*—no manners, eh? But my aloha would kick in and I would simply smile, then talk behind his back later.

ACT LIKE YOU'RE FROM NEW YORK. I don't even care if you are from that place, change your accent, your religion, whatevers, but don't be acting like you in one big *wikiwiki* rush for everything and all arrogant and you need all dis and dat and everyone just so slow here and how do I get anything done. Oh boy, if you like that in Hawaii you asking for one big beef, okay?

CALL ANYONE WITH A TAN "HAWAIIAN." Almost everyone in Hawaii could be classified as *tan*, but guess what? This doesn't mean they are Hawaiian. They may have Hawaiian in them, but they could also be pure or mixed Samoan, Filipino, Tongan, Maori, Latino, African-American, Korean, Japanese, Chinese (do you want me to go on?) and proud of it. Hawaii is classified as "mixed plate." Many Asian/Pacific Islanders are simply called "locals." Don't assume anyone's race without very nicely asking first. Then be prepared to explain your own in detail!

CONSTANTLY REFER TO A GAY MAN AS A MAHU. Although *mahu* is a term that means "gay," it more specifically and commonly is used to refer to local dudes in drag. If you made friends with one big guy with a deep voice named Butch, who's all hairy and leathery and all that, I wouldn't really keep calling him a *mahu* if I were you (especially if you want something from him). And your lesbian friends aren't *mahu*.

MAKE FUN OF THE ISLAND CULTURE. Don't be minimizing the islands' history, satirizing Hawaiian music, commenting on the idle lifestyle or acting like you know more about Hawaii than residents do. And don't mock a hula dancer in front of them, since a lot of those girls are big enough to give you one good lickin', and not the kind of licking you'd prefer!

DISRESPECT ISLAND POLITICS. Many locals have strong feelings about what they perceive as the illegal occupation of the U.S. on their territory (refer to Chapter 1 for the whole complicated story). Okay, Hawaii politics can seem provincial, corrupt, self-serving, overly controlled, slow to change, and out of touch. But have you ever been to any place where it's any different? Really?

DO:
All the DOs are the DON'Ts backwards, okay?

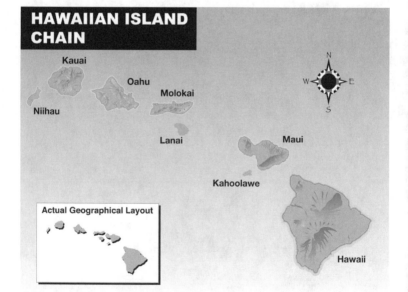

HAWAIIAN ISLAND CHAIN

Kauai

Oahu

Molokai

Niihau

Lanai

Maui

Kahoolawe

N

W E

S

Actual Geographical Layout

Hawaii

HAWAII STATE FACTS

STATE NICKNAME: "The Aloha State"

STATE FLOWER: The Yellow Hibiscus

STATE BIRD: The Nene

STATE MAMMAL: The Humpback Whale

LAND MASS: 6,423 sq. miles/16,635 sq. km (fourth smallest U.S. state)

POPULATION: 1,200,000 est.

HIGHEST POINT: Mauna Kea at 13,796 feet/4,205 m

STATE MOTTO: *Ua mau he ea o ka aina i ka pono* ("The Life of the land is perpetuated in righteousness.")

Visiting Hawaii is not merely hopping off the jet with a lei wrapped around your untanned neck, sunscreen splattered on your nose, and a cute bikini around your loins, then bolting to the poolside for your first of several *mai tais*. Oh no—Hawaii demands much more of you than that. Not only do you have all the hassles of getting anywhere (reservations, transfers, airports, taxi fare, ugh), but once you get here you're gonna have to figure out all the unique ins and outs of gay life in Hawaii as well. The following load of information should get you nicely primed before you even set foot on the islands.

TOURIST SEASONS

Hawaii's tourist season is not surprisingly year round, but mid-winter and early summer is when the retired snowbirds and the nuclear families cram into the state, respectively. Late spring and especially the fall tend to be less frequented months, and room rates may drop during these months—although whenever the kids are out of school, expect a peak in tourist traffic. Another thing to watch out in Honolulu especially is when Japan's national holidays occur (particularly Golden Week, a ten-day period in late April to early May), which can bring a flood of tourists in as well. Christmastime is another popular period for travelers to Hawaii, so book early.

EVENTS NOT TO MISS

OAHU

The annual **AIDS WALK** around Kapiolani Park is in late April (808/521-2437, AidsWalkHawaii.org), and receives a lot of hetero involvement as well. Every two or three years (the next one will probably be in 2009), the all-gay **ATLANTIS CRUISES** (800/6-ATLANTIS, AtlantisEvents.com) does a voyage around Hawaii, usually in late April. When that occurs, usually the circuit-like **VOLCANO PARTY** is held at the same time in Honolulu. In past years it's been held at the Hawaii Convention Center. In April or May, Honolulu is the home of an annual international gay and lesbian tennis weekend tournament, the **ALOHA TENNIS OPEN** (808/222-4709, GeoCities.com/ato_hawaii/ato), which enjoys a good turnout from the community. The Honolulu Gay and Lesbian Cultural Foundation (808/381-1952, HGLCF.org), showcases **THE RAINBOW FILM FESTIVAL** in late May, with lots of gay and lesbian cinema with an Asian accent. Honolulu's **PRIDE** is a rather small affair in late May and early June compared to other Mainland cities. This could be due to the fact that lots of gay residents hop on a plane to L.A. or San Francisco for their June pride fix. However, Honolulu's Pride celebration is growing each year, with over 500 participants at last count. The **GAY & LESBIAN COMMUNITY CENTER** (808/951-7000, TheCenterHawaii.org/Pride_Celebration.htm) puts together a prominent parade from Ala Moana Boulevard to Kapiolani Park, with related festivities at bars and hotels. Honolulu is famous for her hometown enchantresses: there are a number of annual drag pageants, the biggest being often sold-out **UNIVERSAL SHOW QUEEN** (808/372-9350) held every June at the Hawaii Convention Center in Honolulu. **HALLOWEEN** is a surprisingly large public street event, with men in drag and tourists galore packing the sidewalks of Kalakaua Avenue. Just making your way through the few blocks' masses of sweaty bodies may take up a good chunk of the evening.

MAUI

In late September, the **ULTIMATE PANACHE PAGEANT** (808/280-6776, TheDynastyCollection.com) happens in Kihei, where not one, not two, but three crowns are given out to drag queens and a king in an elegant evening event. In early October, join the **WAIHINE'S WYLDLIFE WEEKEND** (808/281-3126, MauiGayInfo.com) in Keanae where womyn enjoy art, music, workshops, games, dancing, spa services, and more. The **MAUI COUNTY FAIR** (808/242-2721, MauiCountyFair.com) in Wailuku also occurs in October and is quite a site, drawing over 90,000 spectators. There are livestock shows for you 4-Her's, rides, great arts and crafts, and live entertainment, but no guys in dresses, since a local drag troupe The Cosmetix was banned from performing one year, causing a local uproar. Tourist haven Lahaina is the spot for the **HALLOWEEN—MARDI GRAS OF THE PACIFIC** (808/667-9194, VisitLahaina.com), where even more drunk people than usual (30,000 or so) stumble around the place, the streets get packed, and the drag queens come out to play. There's a *keiki* (kids') parade in the afternoon before the debauchery. And throughout the year, the **MAUI AIDS FOUNDATION** (808/242-4900, MauiAids.org) has been known to throw fund-raisers and dances, and a good chunk of the community shows up for those.

KAUAI

The **WAIMEA TOWN CELEBRATION** in February (808/338-1332, WKBPA.org), formerly the Captain Cook Fair, includes canoe and foot races, ukulele contests, cotton candy, pig-on-a-spit, games, and lots o' beer—can't get more island style than that! All to help commemorate the landing of that *haole* on Kaua'i (later to be killed on the Big Island). Kauai holds its own 130-mile AIDS bike-a-thon, the **PARADISE RIDE** (808/245-2851, ParadiseRideKauai.com) in August. It's a two-day route that visits both the northern and southern shores of the isle. The nine-day, gay-founded **MOKIHANA FESTIVAL** (808/822-2166, Mokihana.Kauai.net) in late September attracts a lot of local queer participation and spectators, with games, story-telling, lei making, and in particular hula—and a lot of it. The **MALAMA PONO ANNUAL FUND-RAISER** (808/246-9577, Malama-Pono.org) for Kauai's AIDS organization is held in December, with a silent auction and *pupus* (island appetizers) in a ballroom setting.

BIG ISLAND

In August, the Hawaii Island HIV/AIDS Foundation (808/331-8177, HIHAF.org) hosts its annual fund-raiser, the posh **TASTE OF LIFE** event with participants surveying the creations of the island's top chefs and food and wine makers. The **QUEEN LILI'UOKALANI**

LONG DISTANCE OUTRIGGER CANOE RACE (808/334-9481, Kaiopua.org) takes place over Labor Day weekend at the beach in front of the King Kamehameha Hotel. It's the largest race of its kind in the world, attracting over 3,000 participants from 77 international clubs. The weekend closest to the first full moon in October is when all eyes in Kona are on the **IRONMAN TRIATHLON** (808/329-0063, VNews.ironmanlive.com), which begins at the Kailua Pier. A lot of fun, but it is hard to get rooms this time of year since thousands of people normally show up, so be sure to call ahead. The **KONA COFFEE FESTIVAL** (808/326-7820) happens in early November around Kailua–Kona and Kealakekua, with coffee picking contests, coffee farm and mill tours, tasting competitions, and even a healthy baby contest!

MOLOKAI

A good chunk of Molokai's population turns out for the **KA MOLOKAI MAKAHIKI FESTIVAL** (808/553-3673, MolokaiEvents.com) held at the Mitchell Pauole Center in the heart of Kaunakakai in late January. Competitions in traditional Hawaiian games take place such as lawn bowling, wrestling, and spear hurling, as well as lots o' good food and music. It was originally an ancient four-month event honoring the god Lono. For three days in May, the popular **MOLOKAI KA HULA PIKO** festival (800/800-6367, MolokaiEvents.com) erupts in celebration of Molokai as the traditional origin of hula. **PAPOHAKU BEACH PARK** comes alive with food, music, crafts, and excellent displays by proud local hula groups. The **NA WAHINE O KE KAI**, "Women Against the Sea" (808/ 259-7112, NaWahineOKeKai.com) takes place on the last Sunday of September, while the men's race **MOLOKAI HOE**, "Molokai Paddle" (MolokaiHoe.org) takes place on the second Sunday in October. Both depart from the **HALE O LONO HARBOR** on Molokai's southwestern shore. Founded in 1952, the race is a grinding 40 plus miles through the turbulent Molokai Channel to the finish line at Waikiki. Come down to the harbor to cheer on the paddlers in an old island sport that has become super popular and is now televised statewide.

HAWAII WEATHER SYSTEMS

Hawaii will rarely get into the high 90s at any time of the year, and it's the only U.S. state to have never reported a temperature of zero degrees Fahrenheit or below (even though it can snow at times on the highest peaks). Summer is between the high 70s to the high 80s. On the whole, wintertime sees less than a ten-degree dip from summertime. Cool northeasterly trade winds keep the climate temperate and consistent. On winter nights, it can dip down into the 50s, perfect for queer honeymooners. Hurricanes are rare in Hawaii, but the season is technically from June to November. The last major hurricane to hit Hawaii was Iniki, which severely damaged Kauai in September 1992. Keep in mind that winter storms in the North Pacific create huge waves across the state, at times making swimming and snorkeling unsafe.

Given all this talk about consistent weather and all, be forewarned: Variations on any given island will occur a lot. Each island has a dry western side (leeward for you sailors) and a wet eastern side (windward). Between the wet and the dry sides, the climate can be like night and day, from arid desert to dripping jungle. To complicate things, *mauka* regions (up toward the mountain side of an island) are cooler: less three degrees per 1,000 feet. *Mauka* regions are rainier in general than the *makai* regions (down toward the ocean).

To further complicate things, different sides of the island usually have different rainy seasons: The leeward or drier southern and western sides of the islands receive rain in summer, while the windward or northern and eastern sides of the islands see more rain in winter. Fleeting rain showers that come and go before you realize it, called *blessings*, are common in Honolulu. And to complicate things even more, mornings may generally be sunnier than afternoons due to offshore and onshore breezes, and cloud accumulation at the summit of the mountains.

A case in point of all this meteorological madness is the Big Island where almost a dozen earth climates are represented, from monsoonal to periglacial. So like those Boy Scouts told you, Be Prepared.

WHAT TO BRING?

Obviously, Hawaii is usually classified as warm even if you are from Miami, Manila, or Pago Pago. It's no shock that people dress casually here. Not just leisurely, but casually. For residents this means wearing a short-sleeved shirt is dressing up, and a tank top is dressing down (actually no shirt is dressing down). Unless you are here on stuffy Mainland business, dress shoes, jackets, ties, even long-sleeved shirts are almost unheard of, even in Honolulu. High heels, formal dresses, and stockings are not usually worn by women either. So leave those clothes and their uptight attitude behind. The most you will ever need are light slacks and an aloha shirt for the guys, a snazzy sun dress for the gals. Light materials are preferable, and dressing in "aloha wear" with bright island fabrics always looks classy. Shorts, a nice shirt, and tasteful sandals are the norm for most places.

Plan on packing at least some of the following: swim suits (a must, even if you don't know how to swim), shorts, shirts, a windbreaker, some kind of hat for shade, and thick-soled tennis or hiking shoes (for the sharp lava rock). Most sports equipment like masks and snorkels can be rented or purchased on the islands for a nominal fee. Insect repellent and especially sun block are mandatory in Hawaii. The sun on the islands is ferocious, and some Mainlanders can actually get third degree burns if they're not careful.

Although Hawaii is slightly more expensive for consumer items, everything from reef slippers, to disposable underwater cameras, to lava-lava wraps, to water-based lube can be easily purchased here at WalMarts, K-Marts, or the ubiquitous ABC stores. Skimp on things like jeans and heavy jackets, although a light sweater might be handy for higher elevations. Packing everything in one carry-on bag is a good idea, since your clothes will be light and your check-in baggage may very well end up in Bora Bora.

THE PRICE OF PARADISE

As you probably figured, Hawaii is a pricey place to visit, and living's not too cheap here either. Oftentimes, the excuse is that everything needs to be shipped to Hawaii, but that fact is true of other islands and even the Mainland, and isn't Hawaii an easy stop on shipping routes anyway? Others blame price-gouging and high taxation, but whatever the reason don't expect prices to be as cheap on the Mainland for anything (except maybe fresh leis!).

PAYING FOR A ROOM

Most superior mainstream hotels like the Hilton, Four Seasons, and Sheraton can easily run up to $400 a night and beyond into the stratosphere. Most travel agents and package dealers will put you up in independent local hotels, the biggest being the family-owned Outrigger chain. The rate card price for these types of hotels may be anywhere from $100 and up.

Hotel/air/car package trips are really the way to go in Hawaii (especially in Honolulu) if you don't mind staying at a mainstream, straight hotel. Most of the best packages originate from the West Coast. If you happen to have a Hawaii driver's license or have a friend who does, you may be able to snag local's, of course, sometimes half-price *kamaaina* rates. During times when a hotel has low occupancy, they may offer walk-in rates that slash the published price by a third. Some island timeshares present excellent room/car offers in exchange for viewing their property and asking if you are interested in purchasing.

Keep in mind that hotels in room-drenched Honolulu tend to be better priced than elsewhere in the state. Also, it's harder to get discounted rates in the busy winter months. Late spring and fall tend to be better for reductions.

For the gay or lesbian traveler, the humble homo bed & breakfast is the most highly recommended way to experience Hawaii. Not only are you far from the maddening crowd, you get to pick the brain of the built-in local gay information source (the owner). You are also much more likely to meet other gay travelers this way. And what you are getting for the cost of most B&Bs (anywhere from $35 to $250) is a lot prettier than the sometimes disappointing hotels in that price range. Most gay B&Bs have a quiet home-like atmosphere, and many offer pools or spas and wonderful natural settings.

If you are planning on staying longer than a week in any one spot, then check out vacation rental possibilities. There are more empty condos for short-term rent than you realize, and many island homes will lease out their downstairs or *ohana* cottage for a reasonable fee. This works out especially well if you are traveling with a few people and don't want to be climbing up the walls of a tiny hotel room.

EATING OUT

Restaurants tend to be pricey for what you get, especially in the more remote spots of the islands. Expect to pay extra for an ocean view too. Honolulu offers the full gamut of eateries, and fast food and "plate lunch" places can be found all over the state. Hearty plate lunches, which usually consist of an Asian-style meat, some vegetables or macaroni salad, and two scoops of rice, are the substance of choice for locals.

Oddly enough, fresh fish is not particularly cheap in Hawaii. It's also hard to find Hawaiian restaurants that offer traditional island fare like poi or *lomilomi* salmon. Your best bet for these acquired treats is to head to a luau that has been recommended to you by a knowledgeable resident. Thai, Japanese, Chinese, Vietnamese, and even Indonesian restaurants are also abundant in Hawaii. And there are always burgers and steak joints around for the true Mainlanders. Carefully prowl the regional island tourist publications for profitable restaurant coupons found within their folds.

GETTING AROUND

BY AIR With the advent of low cost inter-island airlines in recent years, prices on airfare within Hawaii have dropped dramatically—some even advertising $1 fare specials! However, if you plan to island hop, you may still want to check into a package that includes your Mainland and inter-island airfares all in one price. Keep in mind that island hopping still entails potentially long security lines at the airports, so sticking to one or two islands per vacation is always a good idea.

BY SEA Another brand new development is the opening of inter-island ferries between the islands. Most newcomers are surprised it's taken so long, but for years the only ferry service was between Maui and Molokai and Lanai, but a new company, Hawaii Superferry (877-HI-FERRY, HawaiiSuperferry.com) opened up its first route in 2007, with more opening in 2009, including Big Island to Oahu and Maui, and Kauai to Oahu. Fares may be slightly higher than flying, but the advantage is that you can take your rental car on the ferry as well.

BY LAND Honolulu offers cheap and efficient island-wide transportation. The bus system can even get you to the North Shore for 2 bucks! But don't get excited. Everywhere else in the state, figure on renting a car to see or do anything. Major rental agencies are found at every island airport, although prices are steeper than on the Mainland. Book your rental car well in advance of your arrival, since some outer island airports regularly run out of cars during busy spurts like conventions. Ask if they have free pick-up service to your hotel if you're not renting at the airport. Taxis are a little pricey and hitchhiking is technically illegal, although you will spot a lot of people with their thumbs dangling out on the side of the road.

HAWAII CALLING

Phone calls to the state of Hawaii all begin with the area code (808). But you must also dial the area code whenever calling *between* the islands. Hence, a long distance call. For calls made *within* an individual island, you do not need the area code and the calls are free. This unique system makes the Big Island the largest toll-free calling area in the U.S. So go ahead—reach out and touch someone!

GAY HAWAII TOUR OPERATORS AND TRAVEL AGENTS

Getting a package deal to Hawaii is the way to go. You get breaks on multiple nights at the same establishment, discounts on rental cars, and sometimes breakfast and activities thrown in as well. Some tour agents offer enticing discounts for island-hopping too.

Unless you just adore cities, try not to spend the bulk of your time on Oahu. Each outer island has a distinct character, and merits its own separate trip for exploration. In fact, many savvy return visitors learn to skip Honolulu altogether and instead book direct flights to Maui, the Big Island, or Kauai. Think about staying put in one spot and getting to know it rather than madly taking in every single island in one trip.

BIRD OF PARADISE TRAVEL A gay-owned agency that books airline tickets, hotels and B&Bs (both gay and straight), car rentals, and gay and lesbian tours and cruises. They also have affordable neighbor island packages. P.O. Box 4157, Honolulu, HI 96812. (808)735-9103, boptravel@aol.com

BLACK BAMBOO HAWAII A well-established gay-owned company on the Big Island that can help out with gay and straight

HOT LAVA MEETS THE PACIFIC AT VOLCANOES
NATIONAL PARK, BIG ISLAND

accommodations and retreats, referrals, and car and activity packages for all the Hawaiian Islands. 800/527-7789, (808)328-9607, BLACKBAMBOOHAWAII.COM

HAWAIIG BY ONLY IN PARADISE This concern offers gay activities, lodging, wedding, air, hotel, and car packages, and their Web site includes gay island info, bulletin boards, and chat rooms. Nudist friendly! (800)583-0783, HAWAIIG.COM

PACIFIC OCEAN HOLIDAYS A long-established Honolulu-based gay travel company that can help with gay lodgings, airfare, and car packages on Oahu Maui, Kauai, the Big Island, and even to the mainland. (800)735-6600, (808)944-470, GAYHAWAII VACATIONS.COM

HAWAII'S BEST LGBT WEB SITES

Plan your homo Hawaiian wedding or meet that special local contact without ever leaving the privacy of your own home! Most business Web site addresses in this book are included with the actual listing, but here are some valuable queer Hawaii sites to get you started:

ALOHA.NET/~LAMBDA A gay Kauai Web site with lavender listings, *malahini* (newcomer) info, and event info.

GAYHAWAII.COM Online version of the *Pocket Guide to Hawaii*, with introduction and gay listings for each island, as well as a complete list of links to gay businesses for the state and live chat and bulletin boards. Helpful and popular.

GAYONKAUAI.COM Lovingly hosted by local residents Loyd and Roy, who give Web surfers info on gay events, businesses, reflections, trivia, and personal pages.

HAWAIIGAYMARRIAGE.COM Information and colorful page providing referrals for those interested in same-sex marriage registration, registry forms, related services, as well as a history of the gay marriage struggle in Hawaii and updates on the legal front. Put out by the Gay and Lesbian Education and Advocacy Foundation.

HAWAIISCENE.COM/GAYSCENE One stop shopping for all gay info about Honolulu with some neighbor island info, ads and links to Web sites for gay bars, gay artists, gay travel companies. Extensive and detailed.

LAMBDAALOHA.COM An instructive site for what's going on in queer Kauai, including bulletin boards and info on local beaches and hangouts.

MAUIGAYINFO.COM Run by the local gay group Both Sides Now, this site lists local LGBT events, Maui gay info, and tons of useful gay links.

MAUIPRIDE.COM Another major source of info on what's going on in gay Maui, including a calendar of events, photos, and maps.

ODYSSEYHAWAII.COM You can download an issue of the magazine, get gossip and info on club events, local news items, celebrity interviews, outer island gay listings, nightlife snapshots, and indulge in some rollicking reading like Freddie Jordan's famous column

"The Mouth." And don't worry, you'll find local photo escort ads, with and without faces.

OUTINHAWAII.COM A homegrown site for resident info on Oahu, Maui, Kauai, and the Big Island with local gay news, hot personals, a useful events calendar, bulletin boards, and accommodations listings.

OUTSPOKENHAWAII.COM A local site for gay and lesbian residents of the Big Island, with queer business listings, events calendar, classifieds, and bulletin boards.

OAHU

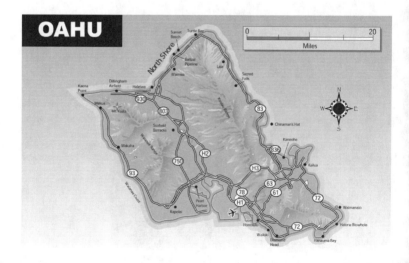

ISLAND FACTS

ISLAND NICKNAME: "The Gathering Place"

ISLAND COLOR: Yellow-orange

ISLAND FLOWER: Ilima

LANDMASS: 597 sq. miles/1,552 sq. km

POPULATION: 875,000 est.

HIGHEST POINT: Mt. Ka'ala at 4,003 feet/1,220 m

RAINFALL: 25 inches/64 cm in Waikiki, 158 inches/401 cm in Manoa Valley

Nearly 75% of the state's population lives on Oahu. It's the site of the only *interstate* highways in Hawaii, and the only royal palace on U.S. soil, the Iolani Palace. The longest river in Hawaii is Oahu's Kaukonahua Stream at 33 miles.

GEOGRAPHICAL OVERVIEW

WAIKIKI refers to the long stretch of cement and steel along one of the world's most justifiably famous beaches. This is where most tourists (gay, straight, or otherwise) reside. Waikiki is roughly outlined on the west and north sides by the Ala Wai Canal, and on the east side by the Honolulu Zoo and Kapiolani Park. The jagged crater of **DIAMOND HEAD** overlooks it all from the east. The peaceful yet sometimes polluted Ala Wai Canal acts as a city moat where you may spot hunky canoe paddlers practicing.

The traditional gay center of Waikiki was up until the late 1990s a unique stretch along **KUHIO AVENUE** between Kalaimoku Street and Lewers Street. Real estate market pressures finally won out, and the funky, queer Kuhio block of old shops and buildings was sold to make way for a modern shopping center. The closed gay businesses in the area were not able to reopen elsewhere. **EATON SQUARE,** an enclosed courtyard-style group of buildings located in a section of northwestern Waikiki, acts as a tiny gay enclave in its stead. Eaton Square has a couple of "private clubs" for gay men and a gay bar, albeit a bit hidden from the main streets.

Honolulu's main gay beach is the appropriately-named **QUEEN'S SURF** on Waikiki's eastern flank. It's near the grand yet currently abandoned 1927 war memorial **NATATORIUM** (just past where Kapahulu Avenue meets Kalakaua Avenue), although there are plans to restore the beaux arts structure. Tourists and *kamaaina* alike gather in the sand of Queen's Surf and on its grassy lawn—you'll know by the Speedos you're in the gay area! The volleyball areas on the grass are where gay groups frequently play. Further east around the point of Diamond Head lays the gay-popular, cruisy **DIAMOND HEAD BEACH**, and **SANDY BEACH** out near the airport runway is also a homo haunt.

The city of Honolulu is by no means merely Waikiki. Head over the Ala Wai Canal on Ala Moana Boulevard, and you'll be out of the clutches of Waikiki and in the grasp of the **ALA MOANA SHOPPING CENTER**. Huge and monolithic, this multi-tiered monument to consumerism is Hawaii's finest, and was the world's largest mall when it opened in 1959. It's a fun place to catch free concerts and hula shows.

Further down Ala Moana Boulevard, you'll hit the conspicuous, gothic **ALOHA TOWER**, for four decades the tallest structure in Hawaii. Its ten stories can be scaled for free for decent views of the city. Tourist cruise ships still dock here as in the olden days (including the Atlantis gay cruises when they're in town), and the area around the tower has been transformed into a tidy shopping plaza.

Many visitors completely bypass the historic **DOWNTOWN**, which is the general area tucked between King and Beretania Streets, behind the Aloha Tower. The district holds many architectural and ethnic wonders. The **IOLANI PALACE** off of King Street is the only royal palace in the U.S. The impressive building was erected by King Kalakaua, known as the "Merrie Monarch" for his fab parties. Sadly, it was also the site of his sister Queen Lili'uokalani's imprisonment after American businessmen overthrew her in the late 1800s. The palace was the state capitol all the way up until 1969, and was restored in the late 1970s to its original splendor. The grand throne room features the original thrones of king and queen, and the Douglas fir floors around the palace are so polished that visitors must wear cute little booties over their shoes for the 40 minute public tours.

OUT TRAVELER RATINGS GUIDE

GAY-FRIENDLY: ▼▼▼
GAY SCENE: ▼▼▼▼
LESBIAN SCENE: ▼▼
PRO-GAY LAWS: ▼▼▼
HIV RESOURCES: ▼▼▼▼

Just north of the palace is the current **STATE CAPITOL BUILDING**. Looking something like a 1960s public library (and a bit grungy for wear), it includes a four-story atrium, a courtyard paved with Molokai sand, two domes meant to represent volcanoes, and water surrounding them to represent islands (you'll get it if you look closely enough). The public is welcome to sit in on Senate and House of Representatives sessions January through April—that's if you really feel like spending your vacation listening to politicians! Check out the strange, squat statue of the revered Father Damien standing in the front of the building. Also visit the **QUEEN LILIUOKALANI STATUE** between the palace and the State Capitol Building. In her hands, the monarch is holding a copy of a revised Hawaii constitution and the hymn *Aloha Oe* (both of which the very intelligent woman penned), and the *Kumulipo*, the Hawaiian chant of creation.

WAIKIKI BEACH, HONOLULU

From the statue, stroll up to the beginning of Hotel Street, which winds its way through the hustling financial and banking district of Honolulu. Just before you see two dragons on either side of Hotel Street, turn right up Bethel Street to check out the restored **HAWAII THEATER**. Art films and frequent gay and lesbian presentations are shown here. Once you pass those dragons on Hotel Street, you'll know by the old-fashioned storefronts, Vietnamese and Filipino eateries, and cluttered Asian supermarkets that you have entered colorful and history-rich **CHINATOWN**.

HOTEL STREET has traditionally been on the seedy side, and once was part of the district dubbed "Hell's Half Acre." It was actually worse off during World War II and thereafter, when numerous brothels serviced our men in uniform. The pink-painted Armed Forces YMCA nearby was a notorious gay meeting point in WWII. Nowadays, upscale eateries, lounges, and art galleries have helped the rejuvenation of the area.

Along **MAUNAKEA STREET** are many lei stands where aunties sit and string some of the best garlands of fresh flowers found on Oahu. It's a welcome scent in all the noisy commotion. The whole artsy, ethnic area of Chinatown is attracting more and more of a homo crowd recently, so keep your gaydar well tuned.

One worthwhile trip out of Honolulu is up the **PALI HIGHWAY**, right behind Punchbowl Crater. This road takes you up the green Nuuanu Valley, where many of Hawaii's royalty are buried at the **ROYAL MAUSOLEUM**. Many historic homes of various architectural interest line this four lane highway, and about halfway up on the south side of the road is the driveway to **QUEEN EMMA'S SUMMER PALACE.** Its interiors are filled with large koa wood four-poster beds, royal feather plumes, and paintings of the alii adorning the walls.

Continue up the Pali Highway, and before you enter the

first tunnel follow the signs for the **NUUANU PALI LOOKOUT** for impressive views of the lush Windward Coast framed by dramatically carved cliffs. The lookout's sheer drop-off is where King Kamehameha infamously forced nearly 400 of the island's warriors over the cliff to plummet to their deaths far below, securing his victory over Oahu.

Head out of Waikiki toward the east on Monsarrat Avenue, and you'll hit **DIAMOND HEAD**. Arguably the most famous landmark in

OAHU Downtown Honolulu

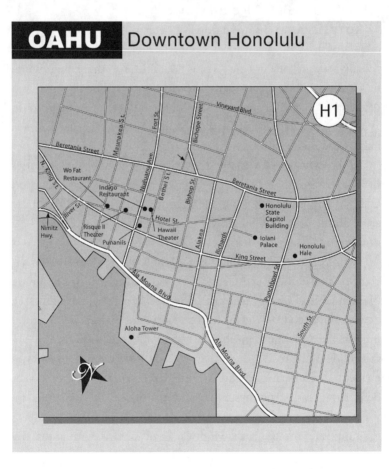

the Pacific, this extinct volcano was named by a group of misguided British sailors who mistook the calcite crystals they found there for gems. The Hawaiians call the crater Leahi instead. Tons of visitors take the time to drive through the tunnel into the crater, where you can hike through military shelters and ramparts to vista points. The absolutely splendid 360-degree views of southeastern Oahu offer a gorgeous perspective on the city.

Drive out of Honolulu eastward on the H–1, and the road will become narrower and change into the Kalanianaole Highway, then lead past **HANAUMA BAY**. Only ten miles from the city, this arid cove offers good snorkeling for the throngs of eager tour buses that flock here.

Further on Kalanianaole Highway is the Halona Blowhole and from there you can view **HALONA COVE**, where that horny beach

THE HONOLULU SKYLINE

FRED WANTS BARNEY

Matt Matsunaga is a U.S. Congressman from Oahu's second congressional district (which includes most of Honolulu), and has been a supporter of same-gender marriage for years. He's even appeared in a couple Honolulu Gay Pride parades— something not many local politicians have done. (Matt's father, Spark Matsunaga, was a beloved U.S. Congressman and Senator.)

Although he has at times played political hot potato with the marriage issue depending on the legislature's mood, he has said this about the same-gender marriage battle: "We recognize that the public wants to decide whether marriage should be between one man and one woman; but why would anyone want to deny fundamental civil rights on the basis of sex? The due process and equal protection clause in our State Constitution clearly prohibits discrimination or denying a person's civil rights based upon race, religion, sex, or ancestry."

Or, as he succinctly put it in 1994: "If Wilma is permitted to marry Fred, but Barney may not marry Fred, then, assuming that Fred would be a desirable spouse for either, Barney is being disadvantaged because of his gender."

That's all fine and dandy, but what about poor Betty?

scene between Burt Lancaster and Deborah Kerr took place in *From Here to Eternity*. Look inland along the highway to make out the **KOKO CRATER**, which tradition tells us is the imprint left by the vagina of Pele's sister Kapo.

Making your way around Makapu'u Point, you'll soon pass a pretty lighthouse and then the **SEA LIFE PARK HAWAII** nearby. Although touristy, the park offers pleasant aquariums and dolphin shows.

Soon you'll spot the longest continuous stretch of sand on Oahu, the nearly 4.5 mile **WAIMANALO BEACH**. The highway then wanders into the bedroom community of **KAILUA**, known for its excellent year-round windsurfing and swimming beach. The H–3 highway that also leads into this area is said to be the most expensive freeway ever built, and many residents tried to thwart its construction for years, but the virgin scenery along its route is breathtaking.

North out of Kaneohe on the Kahekili Highway is the beautiful Valley of the Temples, which is home to the Japanese temple of **BYODO-IN**. This stunning replica of a 900-year-old building in Uji, Japan, is open to the public.

Inching your way up the Windward Coast, the green landscape opens up to the town of Laie, the Mormon heart of Hawaii. The church built the **POLYNESIAN CULTURAL CENTER** here and the Brigham Young University campus nearby. A lot of the Pacific Islander college students work at the PCC, demonstrating authentic crafts and dances from numerous island groups, as well as Pacific architecture and foods.

Past Laie keep an eye out for the popular **SHRIMP TRUCKS,** where motorists pull aside to chow down on the little critters, lunch-wagon style. Past the town of Kawela is the notorious **NORTH SHORE,** with some of the best and most intense surfing on the entire planet. You'll understand why surfing originated in Hawaii when you witness the monstrous, multi-story walls of water plummeting the coastline every winter. Die-hard experts hit the surf along Sunset Beach and Ehukai Beach, the latter being home to the infamous **BANZAI PIPELINE**. The most popular of the North Shore beaches is **WAIMEA BAY BEACH PARK** further south, and parking is typically tight. Waimea holds the record for the biggest waves ever surfed in a competition: over 35 feet tall. Each December is the **TRIPLE CROWN TOURNAMENT,** where surfers from around the world vie for prizes in the six-figures.

The nearby 1,800 acre historical nature reserve **WAIMEA FALLS PARK** is where cliff divers hurdle 60 feet into a waterfall pool five times a day. Exquisite gardens line the valley, which used to be settled by hundreds of ancient Hawaiians.

A few miles further is **HALEIWA**, the main town on the North Shore, filled with surfers and wannabes strolling around the old storefronts. Be sure to stop by **MATSUMOTO'S** tin-roofed general store for some of the best shave ice (Hawaiian snow cones) that the islands offer.

Head west on Highway 930 from here, and then south through

IOLANI PALACE, IN THE HISTORIC DOWNTOWN DISTRICT

SPAMILCIOUS

Hawaii's populace ranks as the number one consumer group in the world for the mysterious Hormel canned meat product called Spam. Invented in 1937 and exploding in popularity in Hawaii during World War II, it's estimated that over 10,000 cans a day are now opened by eager consumers in Hawaii, and you will find more than one Spam cookbook on the shelves of island bookstores. One of the state's most popular snacks? The perfect hybrid of East and West: the Spam *musubi* (a rice cake with Spam filling, wrapped in seaweed—not popular in Japan!). If you're in Honolulu in late April, be sure not to miss the boisterous Spam Jam street festival on Kalakaua Avenue, with nonstop dancing and singing, gorging on Spam jambalaya and Spam tacos, and scooping up of items like Spam baby toys, Spam earrings, Spam flyswatters, Spam tattoos, and Spam bibs.

central Oahu and the military town of Wahiawa, better known as home to the **SCHOFIELD BARRACKS**. It is said to be the largest permanent army post in the U.S. When you hit H–1, head west and it becomes the Farrington Highway. The area is being primed as the next mini-metropolis outside of Honolulu. The highway then heads north along the hot and dry **WAIANAE COAST**, which many folks of Hawaiian, Samoan, Tongan, and other Pacific Islander descent call home. Surfing is also big here, and the **MAKAHA BEACH PARK** holds annual long board competitions in February.

Further north is the **MAKUA** area, with a picturesque and often empty white sand beach. Sadly, Hawaiians living in the area were forced out of their settlements when the U.S. military took over the beautiful valley. The road dead ends again soon after, with Kaena Point in the distance. It's possible to hike the unshaded yet pleasant trail a few miles around this bend, which makes up the western-most tip of the island.

On your way back to Honolulu's city lights, do your patriotic and tourist duty by stopping by **PEARL HARBOR** off Highway 90, where millions of tourists annually visit the *USS Arizona* memorial. Built over the visibly sunken ship, the memorial is a reverent affair, with oil from the vessel still oozing up to the water's surface. There's also a submarine museum, and the recently added *USS Missouri*, on which the Japanese signed their surrender.

OVERVIEW OF THE SCENE AND SCENESTERS

It's obvious that Oahu is technically classified as the *beaten path*. Waikiki as a word has become synonymous with tourists—thousands of them streaming off jets from colder and less welcoming origins around the globe. Sheer concrete reaches toward the clear sky, horns honk above sounds of the soft beach, and steep, dark green mountains stand quietly in the background. It's still one of the most scenic cityscapes in the world.

Honolulu was a thriving new gay mecca in the '70s, where newly liberated homosexuals flocked to the carefree beaches and accepting society. Waikiki was seen as new and exotic then, but almost 40 years down the line with mega-construction, traffic jams, shopping malls, and hoards of vacation-package families, some say the charm is a bit tarnished. Although nowadays gay travelers may be bolder to explore more off-the-track locales, Honolulu still serves as a central destination on your way to the neighbor islands or on to Asia. For singles, it has the only real gay nightlife in the state.

TRANSGENDER POLITICAL PIONEERS

Transgender trailblazer Kim Coco Iwamoto successfully ran for a Board of Education seat in late 2006 and won. She beat two former state lawmakers to achieve the highest office ever for an elected transgendered person in the U.S. "It's a pretty rare feat," admitted Denis Dison of the Victory Fund based in D.C. Board Chairman Randall Yee enthused, "Having Kim on the board will provide a very good perspective and viewpoint."

But the strongest comments came from Kim's father: "As a father, I am proud of all my children when they set goals for themselves that are life-affirming and benefit a greater good. I feel that same sense of pride in Kim Coco."

And that's not the only transgendered person with political aspirations in Honolulu. Tracy Ryan ran for the State Senate in 1996 as a Libertarian candidate. Her platform included the legalization of prostitution, marijuana, and same-sex marriages, as well as less government and fewer taxes. A few days before the election, certain opponents ran a smear campaign against her in the *Honolulu Star Bulletin*, stating that she was "this transgendered man," even though she never hid the fact during the campaign. Regardless, Tracy went home with 31% of the vote—a very high percentage for the local Libertarian Party.

Cozy couples are more emphasized on the quieter outer islands.

Once explored, the city of Honolulu reveals some surprising treasures outside the tourist ghettos. It's full of international architecture, scenic campuses and churches, funky restaurants, eclectic shops, and an astonishing mix of East and West in its peoples and outlook. Access to beaches, hiking trails, bike paths, and lush valleys is extremely easy in this metropolis in paradise.

For queer tourists touching its warm shores, Honolulu can present a dilemma. There's plenty of social tolerance, sun-kissed shiny bods, and let's-have-fun attitude, but quite a limited gay world to run around in. This is despite the number of tourists and the fact that three out of four residents of Hawaii reside here. The 1990s saw a number of gay businesses close or move out of the former gayborhood of Kuhio Avenue. This splintering of Honolulu's gay district meant the loss of synergy within the city's community. A new, equivalent gay area has yet to pop up in its place, despite efforts by entrepreneurs. Add to this the fact that many island gays often head to the Mainland to really come out (and not to mention for the higher paying jobs), and you understand the lack of queer cohesiveness compared to other U.S. cities that are Honolulu's size.

Regardless, Honolulu has been quite the queer pioneer. The oldest gay university organization in the U.S. is the Gay and

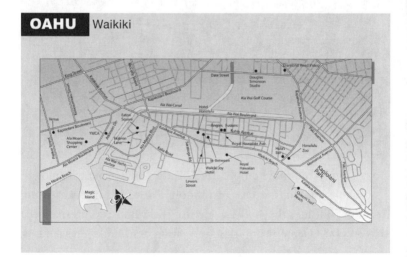

Lesbian Ohana at UH Manoa. The Metropolitan Community Church, Ke Anuenue O Ke Aloha, is over 30 years old, as is the local gay support group. The community also holds a fancy Gay and Lesbian Cultural Festival in the summer. There are gay men's and women's choruses, an annual gay tennis tournament, gay boat cruises, and gay Mormon, Catholic, Episcopal, MCC, Lutheran, and Charismatic groups. And of course, Honolulu was at the trailblazing forefront of the same-gender marriage movement in this country (see Chapter 1).

Honolulu is one of the most gay-friendly cities you'll likely encounter, with few gay bashings, a gay-positive state government, and a generally cordial hetero populace that will treat you and yours with warmth and respect.

Once you crawl out of the city that dominates the island, the rest of Oahu is gorgeous and despite the growing suburbs, fairly rural. On all coasts, Oahu has some of the finest surfing and white sand beaches in the state, as well as dramatic mountains and jagged cliffs. There are lots of hidden natural attractions worth spending a couple days or more to discover, so kick off your shoes, put on your sandals, and hang loose.

TO DO AND SEE

BISHOP MUSEUM Probably the best museum in the world for everything Polynesian (as well as Melanesian and Micronesian), the Bishop is the most famous museum in Hawaii—and worth the hassle of getting to its out-of-the-way location off H–1 on the way to the airport. Unfortunately the crown jewel of the museum, the Hawaiian Hall, housed in a stunning nineteenth century lava-rock Victorian building, is under a $21 million renovation project, slated to reopen in Spring 2008 (but it could be later). No matter—there is still enough to see and do at this impressive complex of museums,

HONOLULU'S BARFLY HISTORY

Back in the swinging '70s, Honolulu's most infamous gay bar was named the Blow Hole, bordering Kapiolani Park on Kapahulu Avenue. Guys would come in off the beach at Queen's Surf, strip down at the bar, and jump into the Blow Hole's large warmed pool, which would be jam-packed by evening's end. The bar and dance floor were on the ground floor of a now-defunct hotel, and in true Waikiki fashion, a grocery store now sits where this Honolulu gay landmark once thrived. As one 1970s survivor describes it, "It was a wild and crazy time, just after the hippy era of sexual revolt, and even when you went to the bathroom, people were mighty free with their hands. People are a little more respectful of each other now!"

If you go back far enough, the big gay bar in the 1950s and 1960s was called The Clouds, on Kapahulu off Kalakaua. It was frequented by the crème-de-la-crème discreet queer community of the time, but went downhill by the '70s. And The Wagon Wheel, near the formerly gay Kuhio block, was gayish even in the 1940s.

History, as always, does indeed repeat itself: In the same proximity to where the ghosts of The Blow Hole and The Clouds dwell, Hula's now operates on the same street overlooking Kapiolani Park, a stone's throw away from Queen's Surf.

including the Polynesian Hall housing rare Pacific culture artifacts, and the Khili Room, filled with royal memorabilia, including the fragile feather standards (used as flags in old Hawaii). The Science Adventure Center sports a huge model of an erupting volcano you can walk through, with plenty of info on the islands' unique and in many cases extinct flora and fauna. 1525 Bernice Street, Honolulu. (808) 848-3511. BISHOPMUSEUM.ORG

DORIS DUKE FOUNDATION FOR ISLAMIC ART The dream of the late tobacco heiress that has only recently come true, opening its door in November of 2002. Ms. Duke had a turbulent and at times unhappy life. She died in 1993 and stipulated in her will that her opulent and fanciful home (called Shangri La) on the shores of Diamond Head be turned into a museum. Now housing her 60 years of collecting more than 3,500 works of art from the Muslim world (many embedded in the house itself), her home is open to small group tours, but you'd better make reservations months in advance due to its popularity. 4055 Papu Circle, Honolulu. (866) DUKE-TIX, (808) 532-3853. SHANGRILAHAWAII.ORG

DOUGLAS SIMONSON STUDIO This native Nebraskan has been a mainstay of the Honolulu arts scene for over two decades. Internationally known for his stunning male nudes in a huge variety of artistic styles (mainly of strapping local young Asian and Pacific Islander men), Simonson's works are priced anywhere from $25 to $25,000, and include posters and calendars. Simonson is happy to arrange private showings at his Date Street studio in Waikiki. (808) 737-6275. DOUGLASSIMONSON.COM

THE LEGEND OF THE HOTEL HONOLULU

The Hotel Honolulu was *the* gay hotel in Honolulu from the early 1980s to its closure in 2000. It adjoined the once-queer block of Kuhio that had shut down in late '90s, and even though it was not linked to the block, and had a change in ownership and renovations, its demise was fated. In the relatively small time span it was open, the "Gay Liberation" movement had evolved tremendously, and the guest books left in the rooms of Hotel Honolulu acted as a random, confidential chronicle of the era.

Each occupant staying in a particular room in turn spilled their guts (almost literally!) onto the worn pages left for others to read. The books recorded happy drawings of rainbows, multi-page essays on relationships, stupid and hilarious poems, addresses and phone numbers left for contacting, vivid narrations of dark drug trips, recountings of sad and remorseful vacations, and of course pages of blow by

GAY LUAU GROUP NIGHT On a beach on Oahu's Leeward coast, join up to 15 other LGBT travelers hosted by gay bar Angles Waikiki on Sunday nights to experience a real Hawaiian luau in a queer environment. Learn how to make a traditional lei, get a temporary Polynesian tattoo, watch the royal court procession, get a load of the underground *imu* oven, and gorge on classic fare like *poi*, *kalua* pork, *haupia*, and *lomilomi* salmon. Transfers included. (800) 583-0783. GAYTRAVELHAWAII.COM

HULA'S SATURDAY CATAMARAN Thirty or more LGBTs hop

THE LEGEND OF THE HOTEL HONOLULU

blow sexual escapades acted out on the hotel's beds, floors, sinks, counters, balconies—some so excruciatingly descriptive you felt like calling the maid for a major spring cleaning before you sat anywhere! After many inquiries, the ultimate fate of these colorful documents remains unknown. The memories of the real Hotel Honolulu will live on forever in the forgotten room journals left for future generations, wherever their destiny has now taken them.

In 2001, Oahu resident and travel writer extraordinaire Paul Theroux, who had knowledge of the gay hotel, published the fictional novel *Hotel Honolulu* (which, despite its gay characters Amo the flower arranger and his gay lover Chip, who unfortunately kills him, has no actual bearing to the gay inn). The novel begins with words perfectly fitting the real hotel: "Nothing to me is so erotic as a hotel room, and therefore so penetrated with life and death."

aboard a catamaran for an hour and a half afternoon sail around Diamond Head, and they even jump in the water if the seas are calm. All that and a complimentary *mai tai* for $20. If you've never had a chance to experience Waikiki from the water, here's your chance to do it the gay way. Sign up at Hula's bar before two in the afternoon. 134 Kapahulu Avenue, Honolulu. (808) 923-0669. HULAS.COM

SKY DIVE HAWAII Jump out of a small plane on Oahu's breathtaking North Shore (near where the TV show *Lost* is filmed), with a professional instructor strapped to you tandem, to take in the plunging views of the reefs and mountains before your chute gently opens on safe land. One of the most dramatic spots to skydive in the entire world. (808) 637-9700. HAWAIISKYDIVING.COM

NIGHTLIFE

ANGLES Upstairs above Kuhio Avenue, with a fun *lanai* overlooking the street action, New Orleans style, Angles is open-air and made up of two small separate bars on either side of the entry stairway. A friendly young staff makes you feel at home, and an inside dance floor borders the *lanai* (live DJ Thursday through Sunday). You will find a decent mix of the homo world here as with most Honolulu bars, with a leaning toward the youthful and possibly straight crowd. At 2:00 A.M. when the bar closes, the crowd migrates across

NUUANU PALI LOOKOUT ON OAHU'S WINDWARD COAST

a passageway to adjoining Fusion Waikiki, Honolulu's only bona fide queer nightclub with strippers and drag shows. 2256 Kuhio Avenue, Honolulu. (808) 923-1130, (808) 926-9766. GAYHAWAII. COM/ANGLES

BLACK GARTER CAFÉ Every Friday night when the womyn take over Downtown's Café Che Pasta restaurant or similar venues and make it "their own perfect world." There's a live DJ, roomy dance floor, appetizers 'til almost midnight, and best of all $2 cocktails and beer from 9 until 10 P.M. Roses and champagne are given out every week to a lucky winner, and even though they are currently looking for new host venues, the party is sure to go on. Men are welcome. For updates call the info line at (808) 737-6446 #2. BLACKGARTERCAFE.COM

HULA'S BAR & LEI STAND Ripping itself up from its decades-old roots under a massive banyan tree on Kuhio in the late '90s, Hula's, the most famous gay bar in the Pacific, is now housed on the second story of the Waikiki Grand Hotel with views of the lush Kapiolani Park and Diamond Head from the 70 feet of open windows. There's a dance floor, DJ, video screens, and a casual lounge feel that attracts a daytime beach crowd. Most importantly, you'll find wet underwear contests happening here, so don't worry. Although gay tourists in tank tops can at times outnumber locals within its walls, this bar is probably the most popular in Waikiki for *kamaaina* (island residents), with a mix of ages and backgrounds, since everyone always ends up here after sunning at the gay-popular Queen's Surf Beach nearby, since happy hour is a good long 10 A.M. to 8 P.M. daily. 134 Kapahulu Avenue, Honolulu. (808) 923-0669. HULAS.COM

LA MARIANA SAILING CLUB You will feel like an in-the-know resident when swinging by this (mainly hetero) retro South Seas kitsch oceanside bar/restaurant, decorated with vintage 1950s and 1960s Hawaiiana like puffer fish lamps, glass sea balls, Don Ho items, movie posters, and other relics rescued from now-closed Waikiki bars. The food is nothing special, but the drinks are generous, there's a piano player, and you'll be far from the tourist masses at this hidden local favorite, located for 27 years on the waterfront of Keehi Lagoon, where even island residents rarely get to. Look for a white sign that has the number "50" spray-painted in black to find it. 50 Sand Island Access Road, Honolulu. (808) 848-2800

LODGING (LGBT)

ALII BLUFFS WINDWARD BED AND BREAKFAST This gay-owned B&B is located on the windward side of Oahu, 30 minutes from Honolulu. The cozy inn is run by a friendly couple. They offer two bedrooms: the Victorian Room and the Circus Room, filled with antiques and teddy bears. Both have private baths, and there's a pool with views of Kaneohe Bay. You've got the run of the house, and even afternoon tea is included. 46-251 Iki'iki Street, Kaneohe. (800) 235-1151, (808) 235-1124. HAWAIISCENE.COM/ALIIBLUFFS
INEXPENSIVE, LESBIAN-FRIENDLY, NUDIST-FRIENDLY

THE CABANA AT WAIKIKI The only real gay hotel in Hawaii (save for B&Bs), the Cabana is a pleasant, relaxing establishment off Kapahulu Avenue near Hula's. The four-story property is gay-owned, and its 15 units are light and decorated in vintage Hawaiiana. Each suite has a secluded lanai, and some also have full kitchen and living areas. Guests are offered an intimate tropical verandah to meet and mingle, as well as a whirlpool, and complimentary continental breakfast and parking is complimentary. The friendly staff will be happy to help you out with local gay info. 2551 Cartwright Street, Honolulu. (877) 902-2121, (808) 926-5555. CABANA-WAIKIKI. COM **MODERATE, LESBIAN-FRIENDLY, KID-FRIENDLY**

LODGING (MAINSTREAM)

HOTEL RENEW Honolulu's first true designer boutique hotel opened in 2007, steps from Waikiki Beach. Designed by acclaimed San Francisco-based designer Jiun Ho, the 70-room hotel has an elegant zen-like quality, where guests enter through oversized wooden doors, and are greeted by water features and stone sculptures, spacious rooms with dark woods, subdued colors, 500-thread count Egyptian Cotton sheets, sliding wall panels, mini bars with special organic products, in-room safes which fit laptops, flat-screen high definition plasma screen TVs, dimmable lighting, and iPod docking capabilities. The hotel's renewal room will offer guests a variety of signature spa treatments, also available in the privacy of guests' rooms. 129 Paoakalani Avenue, Honolulu. (808) 687-7700. HOTELRENEW.COM **EXPENSIVE, PET-FRIENDLY, HANDICAP-FRIENDLY**

THE ROYAL HAWAIIAN The world-renowned "Pink Palace of the Pacific" is an amazing glance into the Hawaii of yesteryear. This traditional Waikiki beachfront getaway for wealthy travelers and Hollywood elite since its opening in 1927, has tasteful if tiny (and yes, pink-hued) rooms, four-poster beds, high ceilings, and massive closets made for shiploads of luggage travelers used to travel with. Everything matches the salmon Spanish-Moorish stucco exterior, right down to the pink bathrobes and towels. The *koa* wood elevators take you down to the historic open-air lobby, and there's free Hawaiian entertainment nightly over ocean views at their Mai Tai bar. Be sure to stay in the older six-story building, not the modern but less fascinating 17-story tower addition on the eastern end of the property. 2259 Kalakaua Avenue, Honolulu. (800) 782-9488, (808) 923-7311. ROYAL-HAWAIIAN.COM **EXPENSIVE, KID-FRIENDLY, HANDICAP-FRIENDLY**

W HONOLULU Tucked away on the quiet far eastern end of Waikiki, removed from Waikiki's hustle and bustle but oh-so-close to Queen's Surf Beach, this classy, low-key property is where queers with taste go to unpack their Prada luggage. Of the 48 rooms, ask for one on the east side with feels-like-you-could-touch-it views of Diamond Head. The place is filled with all the great toiletries, CDs, wide TVs, and elegant furnishings that the W is known for. Their Diamond Head Grill is one of the best eating experiences on Oahu, and not to be missed. 2885 Kalakaua Avenue, Honolulu. (808) 922-1700. STARWOOD.COM/WHOTELS **EXPENSIVE, PET-FRIENDLY, HANDICAP-FRIENDLY**

WAIKIKI BEACH HOTEL This friendly, hip, Technicolor, 800-plus room hotel across the street from the beach has recently remodeled in a fun retro Hawaiian style, with surfboards in the lobby, bright tropical prints in the rooms, flat screen TVs, a huge pool, and free breakfast to-go picnic baskets for the beach. Be sure to check out the '50s-style Tiki Grill with its 30-foot man-made volcano. 2570 Kalakaua Avenue, Honolulu. (800) 877-7666. RESORTQUESTHAWAII.COM **MODERATE, KID-FRIENDLY, HANDICAP-FRIENDLY**

WAIKIKI JOY HOTEL This low-key, 90-room boutique hotel is tucked away in Waikiki, composed of two towers with an Italian marble open-air lobby with fountains. Each room features a *lanai*, in-suite Jacuzzi, complete stereo system, and the executive suites have full kitchens. There's a cafe and restaurant where complimentary breakfast is served, 15-person private karaoke rooms, and a sauna and small pool downstairs as well. The gay-friendly management has advertised in the gay market for years. 320 Lewers Street, Honolulu. (877) 997-6667, (808) 923-2300. RESORTQUESTHAWAII.COM **MODERATE, KID-FRIENDLY, HANDICAP-FRIENDLY**

DINING

EGGS N' THINGS A late-night institution for the famished party crowd for over 25 years (it's only open from 11 at night to 2 in the afternoon). This fast-paced, clanky diner overlooking Kalakaua has menus on wooden boards and gay-friendly waitresses, not to mention lemon crêpes, *mahimahi* and eggs, or macadamia nut pancakes. The *Honolulu Star Bulletin* dubbed their homemade fresh fruit syrup "sinful." There's always a long wait, so you can practice Hawaiian time. 1911-B Kalakaua Avenue, Honolulu. (808) 949-0820. EGGSNTHINGS.COM **INEXPENSIVE**

INDIGO This spiffy restaurant in downtown, right in back of the historic Hawaii Theatre has tasteful Chinese interior that includes red calligraphy lanterns. Or ask for an outside table on the patio, where you can listen to a gurgling fountain along the old brick exterior. Chef Glen Chu channels his Chinese grandmother's recipes into a new fusion Eurasian cuisine, with offerings like Shanghai mahogany duck with soft bao buns roasted and raspberry hoisin sauce, goat cheese won tons with four fruit sauce, or palm sugar-glazed sweet & sour baby back ribs. Live jazz accompanies your dinner. Voted one of the top lesbian-friendly restaurants by *Girlfriends* magazine. 1121 Nuuanu Avenue, Honolulu. (808) 521-2900. INDIGO-HAWAII.COM **EXPENSIVE**

IRIFUNE This one-of-a-kind hole-in-the-wall Japanese restaurant is one of the best finds in Waikiki. In the same family for years, what used to be the entire restaurant is now a waiting room filled with snapshots of friends on the walls (including fan Sigourney Weaver). The main dining room is an eclectic mixture of masks, fishing nets, posters, and a ceiling with glow-in-the-dark stars and planets. The menu is on the wall and the food is scrumptious and excellent value, with dishes like seared sashimi, pork katsu, and the house specialty garlic ahi served in a variety of styles, explained to you by the amiable wait staff. 563 Kapahulu Avenue, Honolulu. (808) 737-1141 **INEXPENSIVE**

HANOHANO ROOM *Hanohano* in Hawaiian mean "glorious, distinctive, or in an elevated position," and you'll know it with the best views of Waikiki being had on this 30th floor restaurant of the Sheraton Waikiki, accessible by a dramatic ride in a glass elevator. A long-time Waikiki restaurant favorite, live jazz wafts around the huge open room as you gaze on twinkling lights while fine dining on escargot with macadamia nuts, nicoise salad with seared Hawaiian *ahi*, or crispy skinned *moi* fish. Broadway star Rocky Brown sings his heart out here on Friday and Saturday nights. It's only open for dinner, and unlike most Honolulu eateries, there's a dress code, so leave the shorts and t-shirts at the hotel. 2255 Kalakaua Avenue, Honolulu. (808) 921-4600. SHERATONWAIKIKI.COM/DE_HANO. HTM **EXPENSIVE**

KEO'S Keo's is a chain of restaurants throughout Honolulu, which includes the Mekong I and II, began by gay restaurateur Keo Sananikone. The flagship 250–seat eatery on Kuhio in Waikiki has a classy bistro feel that includes walls of teak doors that open to the outside and orchids grown on the North Shore by Keo himself (in addition to the herbs, bananas, and other produce he grows). Chosen by both *Bon Appetit* and *Gourmet* magazines as "America's Best Thai Restaurant," Keo's offers an enormous menu, including Evil Jungle Prince (a blend of chicken, lemongrass, coconut milk, and red chilies), green papaya salad, and prawns in sweet peanut sauce. Reservations recommended. 2028 Kuhio Avenue, Honolulu. (808) 951-9355. KEOSTHAICUISINE.COM **MODERATE**

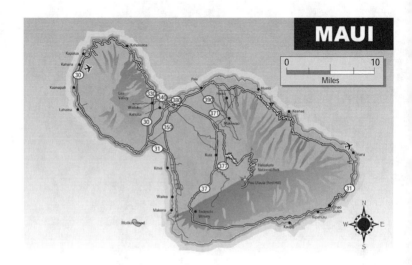

ISLAND FACTS

MAUI IS NICKNAMED: "The Valley Isle"

ISLAND COLOR: Pink

FLOWER: Lokelani

LAND MASS: 737 sq. miles/1,916 sq. km

POPULATION: 141,000 est.

HIGHEST POINT: Mt. Haleakala at 10,023 feet/3,055 m

RAINFALL: 83 inches/211 cm in Hana, 15 inches/38 cm in Lahaina

Maui is the only county in Hawaii to include three islands (with Molokai and Lanai). Haleakala is the largest dormant volcano in the world, and the island holds the last major pineapple and sugar production in the state. The largest banyan tree in the U.S. is in Lahaina, and Maui has the best winter humpback whale viewing in Hawaii along its western coast.

GEOGRAPHICAL OVERVIEW

The adjoining towns of **WAILUKU** and **KAHULUI** sit next to each other on Maui's northern shore like kissing cousins. You will be forgiven if you can't tell where one ends and the other begins. Nearly all Maui's visitors fly into the Kahului Airport, and a good chunk of the island's population resides in these two towns. Where Kahului has the Kmart and Costco, Wailuku has the antique stores and funky restaurants. Although neither town is that touristy, most visitors go through one or the other at some point during their stay.

From the airport heading west toward Kahului, you will pass the **KANAHA BIRD SANCTUARY** on your right, and then come to the Hana Highway. A long strip of shopping malls and businesses line the area, including the humungous three-tiered **KAAHUMANU CENTER** shopping mall (named after the beloved Hawaiian queen). Keep on the road, and a bridge takes you into the older town of Wailuku. Here the aesthetics suit the gay genes better, with charming shops and a plantation-era feel, with the steep verdant West Maui Mountains presenting an eloquent backdrop.

Stroll on **MARKET STREET**, and you will be rewarded with a collection of little antique stores and pawnshops crying out to be explored. The **IAO THEATER** is also on Market, a wonderful piece of Spanish Mission style architecture built in 1928, which sometimes hosts gay plays and musicals.

Up the hill at 103 S High Street you'll spot the **KAAHUMANU CHURCH**, built in 1876. In her always modest style, Queen Kaahumanu pointedly requested that the church bear her name. Treat yourself to hymns sung in Hawaiian on Sunday mornings.

Further up the hill at 2375-A Main Street is the **BAILEY HOUSE MUSEUM**—a must for anyone interested in Hawaii's history. Built by a missionary family from Boston in the early 1800s, there are Hawaiian artifacts on display, a decent gift shop, and none other than one of Olympian Duke Kahanamoku's 150-pound surfboards. If you're lucky, you will also catch local musicians teaching ukulele and slack-key guitar here—can't beat that!

Drive up the **IAO VALLEY ROAD** right behind Wailuku, and (you guessed it), there's a valley called Iao up here. And what a valley it is. Sheer walls of green drama slice into this deep gorge, where King Kamehameha drove the Maui armies up into the valley during his conquest of the island in 1790. It is said the battle that ensued choked the streams red with blood and bodies. On the way up to the valley, you'll pass the **HERITAGE GARDENS** and **KEPANIWAI PARK** with Chinese and Japanese pavilions, a New England missionary home, a Polynesian hale, and a Portuguese garden—"mixed plate," just like Hawaii!

The state park at the end of the winding road will take your breath away. Towering sheets of rock plummet around you, with thin waterfalls making their way to the beautiful stream below. It feels as though you are actually inside an artist's painting. Take the walkway across a small bridge to view the 1,200–foot tall **IAO NEEDLE (KUKAEMOKU)**. This interesting hump was originally a large phallic virility symbol of the god Kanaloa—go ahead and praise it if you need to.

Heading out of Wailuku town north on **HIGHWAY 340**, you will begin the counter-clockwise crawl around the northwest corner of the island. The road gets progressively twisted with blind curves as

OUT TRAVELER RATINGS GUIDE

GAY-FRIENDLY: ▼▼▼
GAY SCENE: ▼▼
LESBIAN SCENE: ▼▼
PRO-GAY LAWS: ▼▼▼
HIV RESOURCES: ▼▼▼▼

you snake up into dry ranch land in the boondocks, passing tiny villages, churches, and a lighthouse. You will know the surf is good when you pass **HONOLUA BAY** because everyone will pull over to watch the near-perfect sets of waves ridden by the near-perfect surfer bodies on boards. On the southern section of the bay is the off-putting named **SLAUGHTERHOUSE BEACH** (there used to be

IAO NEEDLE

one on the cliffs above), which offers some nude sunbathing and bodysurfing.

The quirky road quickly transforms into a super highway, and luxury condos and shopping centers begin to pop up around you. **KAANAPALI** is a planned resort, with uninspired beachfront hotels and run-of-the-mill resorts crammed along the narrow but beautiful (if crowded) beach. And it doesn't really end until you get to **LAHAINA**. Ah, a simple whaling village, you figure. Sorry—Lahaina is tourist central, with the art galleries and shops (selling everything from tacky dolphin sculptures to works by Chagall) along Front Street generally packed. Once the former capitol of the islands and a bawdy whaling center in the early 1800s, Lahaina still holds its charm with antique buildings to explore like the **WO HING TEMPLE** on Front Street. Next to the temple is an adjoining cookhouse showing early Edison films of Hawaii. There's also the historic **PIONEER INN** near the old **LAHAINA COURTHOUSE** and fort remains, and an astonishing **BANYAN TREE** that covers two-thirds of an acre (planted in 1873 and over 50 feet tall with 12 major trunks). Highly recommended is taking a day trip or overnighter to the nearby isle of Lanai on the passenger ferries leaving from Lahaina.

Well-paved **HIGHWAY 30** to Lahaina along the western coast tends to be heavily used since no one wants to drive the slothful Highway 340 from Wailuku. There's a string of small beach parks, with some of the most intense winter whale watching ever. Huge mothers give birth and nurse in the shallow waters straight off the road—watch out for freaked-out motorists slamming on their brakes! You'll soon pass the Maalaea Harbor and its **MAUI OCEAN CENTER** with a good cultural exhibit called "Hawaiians & the Sea" detailing the interwoven bonds the Polynesians have with the Pacific. There's also shark, sting ray, and turtle tanks.

If you keep heading south, you'll hit **HIGHWAY 31** and be on your way to **KIHEI**. This coastline of Maui offers six miles of unbroken beach and near-perpetual sunshine, as well as some of the most tangled growth in the state. Twenty years ago, Kihei was a scattering of houses, with a church or two thrown in. Now it is an unbroken chain of generic condos and mini-malls. But Kihei can be a good area to stay in because of its reasonably-priced condos and vacation rentals (many gay-owned), and its rather central and sunny location. Some Kihei bars and nightclubs host gay nights as well (*see Nightlife*).

South of Kihei is the arid, luxury resort area of **WAILEA**. Its manicured and formal atmosphere stands in stark contrast to Kihei's mishmash of growth. Wailea is where you will find, among others, the Four Seasons, Grand Wailea Resort, and the peculiar, Arabian-style Kea Lani Hotel, complete with white domes and tents and an

BIG BEACH AT MAKENA, MAUI

Aladdin ambience. The world-class resorts are linked by a coastal walking path and excellent beaches, making Wailea one of the most popular lodging areas in Hawaii. Just south of Wailea the road turns and peters out near the excellent, undeveloped **BIG BEACH AND LITTLE BEACH AT MAKENA** (*see To See and Do*). Around this area you'll spot views of the crescent-shaped **MOLOKINI ISLAND** offshore. The remains of this ancient crater make an excellent snorkeling spot, and the hoards of tourist catamarans from Lahaina prove it.

Rewind your way back up toward Kahului again from Kihei on the **MOKUELE HIGHWAY (350)**, and you will spot one of Hawaii's last surviving sugar mills at Puunene, complete with a small museum. Drive east toward Hana on Highway 36, and you soon hit the funky surf town of **PAIA**. Earthy restaurants and shirtless guys with dreads fill the place, with offbeat boutiques and storefronts painted in bright colors. Only expert surfers (or blockheads) venture out into the powerful currents and jagged shore break of **HOOKIPA BEACH PARK**, just past Paia. Here, half a dozen international windsurfing tournaments are held throughout the year that make for an awesome spectacle of athletic prowess.

Highway 36 quickly turns into 360, and you are officially on the **ROAD TO HANA**. Past the town of Huelo, the road becomes famously contorted with over 600 bends as you creep your way to Hana on Maui's eastern tip, and your stomach will count every one. Waterfalls gush down the steep cliffs, pools of all sizes await you on the side of the road, and signs for tropical gardens beckon you. You will be amazed that the road exists at all, being cut directly into the vertical cliffs. With an endless number of one-lane yield bridges, roadside viewpoints, tropical fruit stands, and a slow parade of tourists making the trek daily, the driving pace is like molasses in January. Allow for at least two leisurely hours each way so you can soak up the scenery and practice Hawaiian Time.

Close to Hana is the **WAIANAPANAPA STATE PARK** where you'll be awed by a black sand beach, lava arches, and a short loop trail that will lead you to some amazing ocean-filled caves. Respectful visits can be made to the remains of **PIILANIHALE HEIAU**, thought to be one of the largest ancient temples in the state with 50-foot tall walls, found at the Kahanu Gardens near Hana.

If you follow the highway straight ahead without turning, you'll come upon **HANA BAY**, a salt and pepper beach with local townsfolk hanging out and kids jumping off the pier. Rainy, lush, tiny Hana is the exact opposite of the arid, built-up Lahaina and Kaanapali areas. The sleepy village is full of neighbors waving to each other, island homes with **CHOKE** (lots of) personality, and little tucked away coves. Although Hana does not have any major tourist attractions, do yourself a favor and don't zip to and from Hana like most silly tourists try to do in a dizzying day. Spend at least one night here to savor the beauty and appreciate a sense of what all of Hawaii used to be like.

Instead of winding back to Kahului on the isle's north shore, be adventurous and drive the sparsely populated southern route on the **PIILANI HIGHWAY (31)**. Some people simply describe the highway as "Hell," with rocks, gullies, dust, and potholes adding hearty character to this stretch. The rental car companies usually threaten to kill you if you drive it, but everyone seems to regardless. Once out of green Hana, the terrain slowly becomes drier as you approach the thin tail end of the **HALEAKALA NATIONAL PARK**, where the seven sacred pools (which were actually never sacred and are more like 25) reside at the **OHEO GULCH**. A lot of tourists dip their bodies into the waterfalls and cascading rock ponds (Hint: head to the less-visited upper pools).

Past the gulch, the landscape opens up to sparse desert, and you may miss the little **PALAPALA HOOMAU CHURCH** sitting by itself on the shore. The hunky aviator Charles Lindbergh is buried here, since he lived nearby during the last few years of his life. Now comes the fun part—the already-challenging highway now turns into nasty dirt and gravel. You crawl behind other tourist cars for 4.5 grueling miles. Luckily, there's the wonderful **KAUPO GENERAL STORE** along this stretch, there since 1925 and it looks it. Check out the help-yourself refrigerators and antique camera collection inside.

Forty-five minutes of desolate road with stoic cows under trees, deep lava rock formations, and dramatic views of Haleakala's craggy backside, and you'll ascend into the island's fertile upcountry. You'll soon come upon the **TEDESCHI WINERY**, where you can taste their product in the 1874 King's Cottage tasting room in what used to be an old jail (the colorful King Kalakaua held splendid parties nearby). The winery's pineapple, grape, or passion fruit wines are enticing to repulsive, depending on where your palate happens to reside.

You'll pass a few country villages before the turn-off for **HIGHWAY 377**, which takes you through the sloping residential area of Kula, with great views of West Maui. Turn up **HIGHWAY 378** and you are headed toward **HALEAKALA NATIONAL PARK**— a must for any visitor to Maui. A winding road rapidly ascends past pastureland to the volcano, which last erupted in 1790. Haleakala means "House of the Sun," and this is from where the studly demigod Maui lassoed the sun itself. (Watch out for the mother duck and duckling bicycle tours, where tourists dressed in bright matching outfits speed down the mountain's slope, followed by a bored-looking guy in a truck.) Closer to the summit, the land becomes a barren moonscape. There are some high and impressive lookouts before you get to the main visitor center, which gazes down 3,000 feet into the crater's eerie and awe-inspiring floor. It is

HONOR THY CHILDREN

In 1997, Maui residents Jane and Alexander Nakatani helped in the publication of their incredible family story, *Honor Thy Children*, written by Molly Fumia. Having started their family in California, the Nakatanis imagined an idyllic future with their three sons. However, life is never that simple. Sadly, each one of their three young sons died tragically before his time. The eldest and youngest sons, both of whom were gay, died of AIDS while the middle son was shot to death in Los Angeles. Their powerful story of overcoming tragedy and shame was not easy to share, and since publication they have become beloved supporters of LGBT causes in Hawaii, becoming role models especially to local non-white families trying to come to terms with their gay and lesbian children.

said the whole island of Manhattan could fit into this crater, with no building tops poking over the rim. Drive up to the octagon building at the **PUU ULAULA SUMMIT**. This is the highest point on the island at 10,023 feet. On a clear day, you might be able to see every island but Kauai from here. The park is open 24 hours a day, and many make the pilgrimage to view the delicate colorful sunrise, but be sure to bring something (or someone) warm and call ahead (808) 572-7749) for weather conditions.

MAKAWAO is one of Maui's main upcountry towns along Haleakala's north slope, off Highway 365. It's an interesting New Age/cowboy hybrid of a village that has a number of gay residents. Holistic healers pass ranch hands in the streets, and revamped western storefronts accommodate health food stores and feed shops.

OVERVIEW OF THE SCENE AND SCENESTERS

Maui as a word conjures up all the mystic allure of the Hawaiian Islands as a whole. After Oahu, it is the most frequently visited of the islands, and you will know it by the unending stretch of hotels elbowing the strip of beach in Kaanapali. Condos and mini-malls do the same thing in Kihei, leading to what some call the "Californication" of the island. Now having made that ugly statement, don't be scared—the power of the raw island still surges through. There's a rustic upcountry, remote and pristine Hana, and a rugged and unpopulated southeastern coast, and enough good ole' fashioned *aloha* to make up for all the Best Westerns and Embassy Suites they throw at the place! Maui may seem a bit more homogenized than the other more pastoral neighbor islands, but its infinite beaches, dramatic valleys, twisting roads, and funky towns feel oh-so-true to what the essence of Hawaii really is.

The gay and lesbian scene on Maui is the second largest in the state, although still tiny compared to Oahu's. The island seems to attract a constant influx of our gay family, with most of the socializing happening at the nude Little Beach at Makena and numerous community events. Maui does not have a bona fide gay bar—both of Maui's long-standing venues, Hamburger Mary's and Lava Bar, closed their doors in 1998, and a hopeful gay venue, Jabba's, opened in 2002 and closed in early 2003. Some cite the lack of community support for the closures, others say that Maui is so integrated anyway that a gay bar isn't really needed.

The only gay newspaper on the outer islands, *Out in Maui*, closed shop in 2002 as well. Michael Healey, a board member of the gay group Both Sides Now that ran the paper, explained people move to Maui "to get away from the night life. They're burned out on it." He also described Maui's gay community as "quiet," and that might simply be the answer right there.

But don't completely write gay Maui off yet. Both Sides Now still hosts whale watching, pot lucks, and snorkeling trips for the community that attract scores of local gays and lesbians. On top of that, a handful of bars and restaurants in the Kihei area hold "alternative nights" as well.

The Kihei area tends to be where most gays reside and play. There's a gay following upcountry around Makawao as well. A chunk of gay B&Bs are located east of Kahului, in the pretty Haiku and Huelo areas. The island has its own drag group, the Cosmetix, and a number of same-sex wedding services to choose from.

TO DO AND SEE

LITTLE BEACH AT MAKENA About one mile south of the Maui Prince Hotel in Wailea on the island's southwest coast, turn into the first paved parking lot, taking all your valuables out of your car,

THE ROAD TO HANA

and trek toward the water to behold the spectacular Big Beach. No buildings spoil the 3,000-foot stretch of yellow sand, which is everyone's favorite beach on Maui. Climb north to your right, up the trail on the rocky outcrop and you'll spot Little Beach resting peacefully along the ocean. Gay sunbathers place their towels to the north, and usually slightly outnumber the straight sunbathers. Nudity is the norm, although technically illegal. It's quite a social spot, with both locals and tourists meeting and gawking. By all means, don't miss the impromptu beach sunset drum circle and dancing on Sundays—a Maui must! Makena Road, Makena State Park

OCTOPUS REEF This great dive company is run by the experienced (and out) team of Lynn and Rene, who have lived on Maui for over a decade and have done over 6,000 dives in her waters! They offer unique underwater adventures, including introductory dives, four-day diver certification, shore dives, night dives, boat dives, and any other kind of dive experience you can think of! (808) 875-0183. OCTOPUSREEF.COM

OLD LAHAINA LUAU This beachfront luau just north of Lahaina town takes great pride in presenting an evening of authentic Hawaiian culture, food, and loving and reverent hula dances, a cut above the other more cheesy luaus around the state. You get the flower lei greeting, presentation of pork coming out of the *imu* underground oven, an open bar, and local craftsmen and women creating traditional works before your eyes. The setting is poetic, on the shore under palm trees, with traditional styled buildings and an open-air mood. Both the luau and its sister business, the nearby Aloha Mixed Plate cafe, are partly gay-owned. 1251 Front Street, Lahaina. (808) 667-1998. OLDLAHAINALUAU.COM

5

OPEN EYE TOURS AND PHOTOS Gay guide Pono Fried, an extremely knowledgeable guide and teacher of Hawaiian culture, reveals the unseen Maui to you on privately-guided tours. Pono tailors educational and nature outings to each individual's needs,

THE MACADAMIA NUT IS KING

covering the island's evolution, medicinal and cultural plants (with seasonal sampling of fruit and other edibles), language, history, and legends. It's a great way to get a unique glimpse of Hawaii you may have never seen, and he does tours on Maui and all the islands, with or without walking. Pono is also a published professional photographer, and can take excellent photos of you in dramatic natural settings. (808) 572-3483. OPENEYETOURS.COM

ULALENA Named after the fabled wind and the red-yellow colored twilight rain unique to Maui, named in the Kumulipo (the ancient Hawaiian creation chant), this highly produced and impressive show at the Maui Theatre is a must for any visitor interested in Hawaiian mythology, history, and culture. Cirque du Soleil meets Polynesia in this state-of-the-art multimedia experience, with 20 actors and dancers blending hula and chants with modern dance and acrobatics on a stage built in Montreal and shipped piece by piece to Maui. The larger-than-life musical story touches upon Hawaiian gods like Pele, the arrival of the first Europeans, and the harsh lives of the plantation immigrants. A beautiful and moving way to understand the story of Hawaii from the Hawaiians' point of view. 878 Front Street, Lahaina. (877) 688-4800, (808) 661-9913. ULALENA.COM

NIGHTLIFE

LIQUIDS NIGHTCLUB & GRILL Liquids is housed in the former space of Hapa's nightclub, which was Maui's largest live music club and a long-time local favorite. Hapa's was the site of the popular Ultra Fab Tuesdays aimed at LGBT residents, and Liquids will carry on the queer tradition with a classy (read: dress code) Ultimate Tuesdays, with live DJs, door prizes, and the monthly Dynasty Revue drag show. 41 East Lipoa Street, Kihei. (808) 875-0880

TIP UP TAVERN Having recently changed hands, Bocalino's is now the Tip Up Tavern, a mellow gay-friendly restaurant/bar in Kihei that hosts the Priscilla Club from 6 to 9 P.M., a casual lounge-y happy hour gathering with emphasis on conversation and meeting new friends in a convivial space. "Ono grinds" and Priscillatinis are served during this new Maui get-together. 1279 South Kihei Road, (808) 874-9299

PARADICE BLUZ This basement "underground" space is Maui's latest attempt to up its club scene, with hot DJs and live music as well, booth seating, a redbrick speakeasy atmosphere, "booty contests," and comedy shows depending on the night. Definitely, young, hip, and straight, but this hopping venue is as good as Maui's often dead-on-arrival nightlife gets. 744 Front Street, Lahaina, (808) 667-5299. PARADICEBLUZ.COM

LODGING (LGBT)

MAUI SUNSEEKER The only real gay hotel outside of Honolulu, Maui Sunseeker is made up of 16 rooms on two properties across from the four-mile long Mai Poina Oe Lau Beach in North Kihei. Units are clean and comfy with private baths, satellite TV, and a roof-top, clothing-optional sun deck and two hot tubs, with some workout equipment and an Internet station to boot. Some rooms have lanais and kitchenettes, and the management can help arrange same-sex weddings and private massages. 551 South Kihei Road, Kihei, (800) 532-6284, (808) 879-1261. MAUISUNSEEKER.COM **MODERATE, NUDIST-FRIENDLY, HANDICAP-FRIENDLY, PET-FRIENDLY**

TWO MERMAIDS B&B This lesbian-owned private B&B conveniently located in South Kihei caters to women, gay guys, and straight people. Two bright suites are decorated with tropical fish and flowers, and there's a private Jacuzzi, lanai, and access to a swimming pool. The Kamaole Beach Park III is a short walk down the hill. Enjoy a fresh island breakfast in your suite anytime you want—you're on no clock in Maui! 2840 Umalu Place, Kihei. (800) 598-9550, (808) 874-8687. TWOMERMAIDS.COM **MODERATE, KID-FRIENDLY**

LODGING (MAINSTREAM)

GRAND WAILEA RESORT, HOTEL, AND SPA This oceanfront resort (part of the Waldorf Astoria collection) shows off its price tag of over $600 million with over 40 acres, 780 rooms, five restaurants, 12 lounges, a 50,000 square–foot health spa (regularly named one of the top ten spas in the U.S.), and a $15 million water playground with nine free-form pools on six levels and the world's only water elevator. And every minimum 640–square foot room has three telephones. This addition to the Wailea resort area is as grandly extravagant as Hawaii gets (only outdone by the ostentatious Hilton Waikoloa on the Big Island). 3850 Wailea Alanui Drive, Wailea. (800) 888-6100, (808) 875-1234. GRANDWAILEA.COM **EXPENSIVE, KID-FRIENDLY, HANDICAP-FRIENDLY**

HALE HOOKIPA INN An historic craftsman's style home, built in 1924, this quiet inn has loads of upcountry charm. With high ceilings, wooden floors, two separate wings, and antique furnishings, you feel like you stepped back into the Hawaii of yesteryear. Three rooms (named Rose, Jasmine, and Hibiscus) are outfitted with modern conveniences, and there's a two-bedroom suite with a claw-footed bathtub. The warm-colored interior is complemented by the colorful gardens and majestic trees around the property. 32 Pakani Place, Makawao. (877) 572-6698, (808) 572-6698. MAUI-BED–AND–BREAKFAST.COM **MODERATE, HANDICAP-FRIENDLY**

HOTEL HANA MAUI Maui's first resort in 1946, and completely restored in 2002, this elegantly luxe inn, made up of plantation-style bungalows (697 to 1,475 sq. ft.) on a picturesque hillside, has an enchanting restaurant and bar, ocean views, and an adjoining local art gallery. It's a very special, secluded place: all colors, textures, and materials used on the property are indigenous to Hawaii, and some of the hotel staff has been with the hotel for four generations. The hotel hosts hula shows every Thursday and Sunday, and their Honua Spa with aquatic therapy pool and lava rock whirlpool takes advantage of views of Hana Bay. 5031 Hana Highway, Hana. (800) 321-HANA (808) 248-8211. HOTELHANAMAUI.COM **EXPENSIVE, KID-FRIENDLY, HANDICAP-FRIENDLY**

ROYAL LAHAINA This is an ample oceanfront resort on 27 acres in Kaanapali, with over 333 rooms in a 12 story tower and 114 surrounding cottages, with three swimming pools, two restaurants, and tennis courts. It's a pleasant, if somewhat enormous affair, that recently received $33 million in refurbishments (each room received a $100,000 luxurious makeover). The place is also known for its popular oceanfront nightly luau. 2780 Kekaa Drive, Kaanapali. (800) 222-5642, (808) 661-3611. HAWAIIHOTELS.COM **EXPENSIVE, KID-FRIENDLY, HANDICAP-FRIENDLY**

DINING

A SAIGON CAFÉ When asked for a good place to eat, nearly every resident of Maui will automatically point you to A Saigon Café in Wailuku. Deliciously absent of tourists (and even lacking a sign), this no-frills diner is always packed to the gills with hungry islanders scarfing down beef noodle soup, chicken and vegetable clay pots, and other low-cost Asian yummies in Jennifer Nguyen's

family-style eatery. 1792 Main Street, Wailuku. (808) 243-9560.
INEXPENSIVE

GERARD'S This is a classy, gay-owned restaurant located at the elegant Plantation Inn tucked behind Front Street. You can sit in the garden, on the verandah, or in the downstairs of the old Victorian home. The wicker chairs and antique wallpaper evoke a bygone era. Voted "Best Chef on Maui" for three consecutive years, French owner and chef Gerard offers sumptuous fare like shiitake and oyster mushrooms in puff pastry, ahi steak tartare with taro chips, and fresh Kona lobster with avocado salad. And don't forget the award-winning wines and homemade mango and guava sorbets. Not badly priced for the quality. 174 Lahainaluna Road, Lahaina. (877) 661-8939, (808) 661-8939. GERARDSMAUI.COM
EXPENSIVE

MAMA'S FISH HOUSE If you're looking for a tucked-away beachfront restaurant that feels like a secret, head to Mama's Fish House. Situated on its own private cove on Maui's northern shore, the restaurant has been popular with Hollywood celebrities for years who chow down on dishes like ono fish with fresh coconut, macadamia nut crab cakes, and Polynesian lobster soup. The restaurant's interior feels like an old South Seas beach house, with bamboo walls and lauhala-lined ceilings, and the fresh fish is brought by boat right up to the restaurant daily. 799 Poho Place, Paia. (808) 579-8488. MAMASFISHHOUSE.COM **EXPENSIVE**

KAUAI

N
W · E
S

Secret Beach
Kilauea Point
Princeville
Hanalei
Kee Beach
Na Pali Coast
Kilauea
Kalalau Valley
Donkey Beach
Alaka'i Swamp
Polihale
State
Kokee
State Park
Kealia
Waimea
Canyon
Mt. Waialeale
Pacific
Missile
Range
Mt. Kawaikini
Kapaa
580
Wailea
56
Lihue
550
Kekaha
Waimea
50
550
Koloa
Hanapepe
540
Lawai
Poipu
Spouting Horn

0   10
Miles

ISLAND FACTS

KAUAI IS NICKNAMED: "The Garden Island"

ISLAND COLOR: Purple

ISLAND FLOWER: Mokihana

LAND MASS: 552 sq.miles/1,435 sq. km

POPULATION: 56,000 est.

HIGHEST POINT: Mt. Kawaikini at 5,243 feet/1,598 m

RAINFALL: 21 inches in Waimea/53 cm, 85 inches/216 cm in Princeville

Kauai is the geologically oldest of the major islands. Its Mount Wai'ale'ale has been classified the wettest place on the earth with a killer average of 444 inches a year. Kauai has more miles of sandy beach (nearly 40) than any other Hawaiian island. The state's largest beach is 15 miles from Polihale to Kekaha. Kauai was the first island explored by Captain Cook in 1778.

GEOGRAPHICAL OVERVIEW

LIHUE, the main town on the island's eastern coast, is a grown up plantation village with some interesting architecture and a local business feel to it. It's the main point of entry for most visitors to Kauai, and the seat of county government.

Stroll along the main drag of Rice Street, and you'll see the Spanish stucco-style main post office and the **KAUAI MUSEUM.** Housed in a black lava rock exterior, this excellent museum offers an in-depth overview of Kauai's and neighboring Niihau's history, with everything from illustrations of Kauai's extinct volcanoes, to missionary quilts to necklaces made out of braided human hair.

Just outside of Lihue on Highway 58 follow the signs for the **MENEHUNE FISHPOND LOOKOUT** along the bend of the Hule'ia Stream. A perfectly preserved aqua culture pond sits far below, evidently built by the legendary race of fairies. If you head west back on Highway 58, keep your eyes peeled for the **GROVE FARM HOMESTEAD,** a preserved farmhouse from 1800s plantation life. The Wilcox family's canes, hairbrushes, and even clothes are on display and two housekeepers bake cookies and make mint iced tea for the tour groups

Working north from Lihue on the scenic Highway 56, turn *mauka* (mountain side) at Highway 583 (Maalo Road) to experience the *Wailua Falls.* TV addicts will instantly shout out "Da plane! Da plane!" when they see the 80-foot falls, since they were used in the opening credits of *Fantasy Island.* The cliffs once acted as a diving platform for daring chiefs, but seems they lost a few along the way, since a sign now proclaims "Slippery rocks at top of the falls. People have been killed."

Back on Highway 56 going north, you will pass a golf course and then just south of the Wailua River is the **LYDGATE BEACH PARK**, with a pleasant grassy area and a long, narrow beach. This was once the site of a *puuhonua* or place of refuge for *kapu* law breakers.

Further on Highway 56, you will drive over the **WAILUA RIVER**, where, since 1946, barges take tourists up to the **FERN GROTTOS**. A band plays Elvis' "Hawaiian Wedding Song" as you are hauled up river to see the fern-covered cave.

Next, take a left up Highway 580 for views of the winding river, and check out the *heiau* (Hawaiian temple) remains, as well as the **OPAEKAA FALLS** on the opposite side of the road. This highway takes you up into the residential Wailua Homesteads. The road ends at the beautifully peaceful **KEAHUA ARBORETUM** where you could take a dip (non-skinny) in the cool mountain stream, complete with a rope swing!

Back on Highway 56, a little ways up and you're in the resort area of **WAILUA**. This area blends right into **KAPAA** as you head north, creating Kauai's main tourist universe of shops and restaurants. Since Kauai has no complete circle-island highway (although there were original plans to build just that), the backtracking of cars around here gets mighty cramped at certain times, making for rush hour in paradise. On the ocean side of the highway is the **COCONUT PLANTATION** development, which includes a handful of hotels and a low-key outdoor shopping mall with funky souvenir shops and eateries next door. Be sure to check out the views of the **SLEEPING GIANT** on the nearby mountain ridge from around here—living or

6

KAUAI

OUT TRAVELER RATINGS GUIDE

GAY-FRIENDLY: ▼▼

GAY SCENE: ▼▼

LESBIAN SCENE: ▼

PRO-GAY LAWS: ▼▼▼

HIV RESOURCES: ▼▼▼▼

more like dead proof of what happens when a large man eats too much poi at a luau, or so the legend goes.

Once you exit the town of Kapaa heading north, the crescent-shaped **KEALIA BEACH** pops up on your right. This splendid spot is the site of the weekly LGBT community bonfire. Further north near mile marker 20 is the Koolau Road turnoff for the nudist-popular **LARSEN'S BEACH (KAAKAANIU)**, whose northernmost end attracts a smattering of gays.

Next on the highway you'll go through the scattered village of Anahola. Then the road floats past rich green pastures, some stunning mountain towers and unhurried countryside on your way to the village of Kilauea. There's also the **GUAVA KAI PLANTATION VISITOR'S CENTER** for anyone who is just dying to know more about this tropical fruit.

Take Kolo Road through the town of Kilauea to Kilauea Road, and half a mile later you will be at the **KILAUEA POINT NATIONAL WILDLIFE REFUGE**. The point makes a picturesque site for humpback whale watching in the winter months, with a 1913 lighthouse, thrashing waves, and an emerald sea completing the postcard picture. The refuge is a haven for many nesting birds such as albatross, nenes, and red-footed boobies.

Back on the Highway 56, just before the 24 mile marker is the first turn-off for Kalihiwai Road, along which you will find the parking lot and trail to **SECRET BEACH**, another nude beach that attracts a crowd of surfers and hippies and some gays. Further on the highway, a bridge curves over the pretty Kalihiwai Stream and soon the Princeville Airport is on your left. Turn at the signs for **PRINCEVILLE**, and a manicured road will take you over 11,000 acres of ornate statues, fancy townhouses, and then bring you to the posh **PRINCEVILLE HOTEL** (*see Lodging*). From here, you can see the striking **MAKANA MOUNTAIN RIDGE**. The range is still referred to as Bali Hai ever since Bloody Mary sang to them here in the 1958 film *South Pacific*.

Just past the Princeville turnoff there's a shopping center, and across the road is the **HANALEI VALLEY LOOKOUT**. The bird's eye view from here looks on to the lush patches that produce two-thirds of Hawaii's commercial taro (the native yam–like plant used to make the staple *poi*). The valley acts as a national wildlife refuge as well. The road then winds down the valley to the town of **HANALEI**. Casual and laid back despite the tourists, the village features an old schoolhouse converted into a shopping plaza along the main road. Some nice beach parks line the town's crescent bay. As you leave Hanalei, the **WAIOLI MISSION HOUSE MUSEUM** is on your left. Built by the Alexanders (who didn't fancy the thatched hut they were residing in), the house holds some interesting early 1800s furnishings and woodwork and the best part is the admission, which is free.

The road out of Hanalei is gloriously winding and serene. It crosses many one-lane bridges where you must take polite turns yielding. These bridges along the highway have been kept narrow for a purpose: to frustrate big development, and it's worked. You'll twist past many island homes and tiny beach coves. No self-respecting queer will pass up the chance to pull over at **LUMAHAI BEACH** (not well marked) to follow in Mitzi Gaynor's footsteps to "Wash that man right out of my hair." The water here is often dangerous for swimming, but it's a nice beach for exploring.

Off the highway past the micro-town of Haena is the **MANINIHOLO DRY CAVE**, an eerie football-field-sized cavern acting as a perfect refuge from the North Shore's constant drizzle. At the end of the highway is the legendary **KEE BEACH**, a popular snorkel spot laid out exquisitely at the beginning of the **NA PALI COAST**. A rocky trail up the western end of the beach takes you to a famous hula *heiau* ruin. It was here where hula apprentices had to swim across the shark-infested waters and chant above the roar of the ocean at the temple to become teachers—talk about tough internships!

Many tourists end up at Kee Beach to try their luck at the slippery **KALALAU TRAIL**, an 11 mile trek that leads to the magnificent Kalalau valley. But a shorter hike on the Kalalau Trail will quickly give you gorgeous views of this remote coastline. No matter how you do it, the Na Pali Coast must be seen—whether you choose a helicopter, boat, or hiking tour. Home to many Hawaiians up to the 1800s, the stunning area has few inhabitants now.

Rewinding your way back to civilized Lihue again, head south

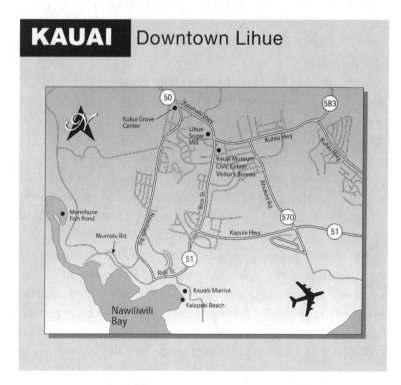

KAUAI Downtown Lihue

6

to Highway 50, where you will find the **KILOHANA PLANTATION** just beyond town. This 1930s Tudor-style mansion has been restored as an upscale shopping spot. The bedrooms, closets, and even toilets and bathtubs of the former home act as store displays for artwork, antiques, clothing, and handicrafts. There are over 35 acres, a working farm, a restaurant called Gaylord's (*see Dining*), and a poofy Clydesdale-drawn carriage for rent to round out the picture.

Past Kilohana you'll see the *makai* (ocean side) turn-off for Highway 520, heading south toward the area of **POIPU**. You'll pass through a long tree tunnel of swamp mahogany along this stretch of road, which will lead you to the cozy plantation/tourist town of **KOLOA**—site of Hawaii's very first sugar plantation in 1835. Three miles later is the arid resort area of Poipu. If you head west on Lawai Road after you pass the Poipu Plaza, you will see the visitor's

KAUAI'S NA PALI COAST'S REMOTE BEACHES

SONS AND LOVERS

On Kauai in the late 1930s, Robert Allerton and his lover
John Gregg Allerton began to transform a 100-acre estate
in the jungle into an amazing garden showplace. The estate
was originally started by Queen Emma, the wife of King
Kamehameha IV, as a royal vacation spot in the 1870s. Robert
and John spent 20 years planting rare and beautiful varieties
of flora on the lush property, sometimes scouring islands in
the South Pacific for certain species. Today the **ALLERTON
ESTATE**, along with the adjoining **NATIONAL TROPICAL
BOTANICAL GARDEN** (808/742-2623, NTBG.org, two
and a half hour group tours Monday through Saturday
tours are $35 per person), is one of the premier botanical
gardens in the country, with sweeping gardens, reflecting
pools, and comely statues. However, most tourists are told
Robert Allerton and his son developed the property, not his
homosexual lover. This is because Robert legally adopted
the younger John with some strings pulled by Robert's
prominent family in Chicago, the result being John officially
changing his name to John Gregg Allerton and the historical
homo slate wiped clean.

center for the **NATIONAL TROPICAL BOTANICAL GARDEN AND
THE ALLERTON ESTATE** (see sidebar). Here they pick you up
for a tour of one of the premier botanical gardens in the country,
developed by Robert Allerton and his lover John Gregg Allerton.
Just past the visitor's center is the queerly named Spouting Horn
blowhole where the ocean rushes into a lava tube and a the ocean

spurts up while a groaning sound emits that is said to be a giant lizard trapped inside.

Head back east into Poipu to find the scenic **POIPU BEACH** which was ripped apart by 30–foot waves and 180-m.p.h. winds during Hurricane Iniki in 1992. It's now a great series of beaches intermittently interrupted by rocky points, with some of the best swimming and bodysurfing on the island. A long line of rebuilt condos and hotels, including Hyatt and Sheraton, elbow each other along the sunny coastline.

Back on Highway 50 past Lawai is the village of **KALAHEO**, a sleepy old settlement descended from Portuguese fishermen and cane workers. The scenic point after the 14 mile marker offers a deep view into **HANAPEPE VALLEY** and the red cliffs beyond. A large chunk of the land in these parts is owned by the Robinson family, the ones who count the island of Niihau among their possessions (see Chapter 10).

Continuing on Highway 50, you will hit the largest town in west Kauai, **WAIMEA**. This was the site of Captain Cook's first landing in Hawaii, and you'll know it by the statue of the *haole* dude on the side of the road. A handful of cute shops and businesses line the highway. Turn up Menehune Road next to the Waimea fire station to behold the **MENEHUNE DITCH**: a three-foot wide, watertight aqueduct built by the legendary race of little people (did someone say fairies?).

From here, take Highway 550 to wind your way up to **WAIMEA CANYON**. The road twists and turns a zillion times as your ears pop open, and the foliage goes from barren to forested as you ascend. The first major canyon viewpoint you hit, **WAIMEA CANYON LOOKOUT**, is the grandest one, looking down 3,000 feet. When you peer down at the gold and maroon vertical walls, terraces, and winding crevices below, you will know why Mark Twain dubbed the canyon with the perfect marketing slogan, "The Grand Canyon of the Pacific."

Keep on heading up the road, and you will be in the **KOKEE STATE PARK**, with a small museum of flora, fauna, and weather displays that includes a nasty continuous video of Hurricane Iniki ripping the island apart.

For you nature lovers, over 45 miles of hiking trails start from around here, and don't you turn your car around yet. The road goes past the stunning **KALALAU LOOKOUT** to magnificently end at the **PUU O KILA LOOKOUT**. Both of these vista points gaze down into the magical Kalalau Valley, which looks like something out of an artist's dream. The sheer green walls and tall rock spires reach magnificently toward the heavens. This is where they finally

KAUAI'S WAIMEA CANYON

decided not to build a continuous highway to the North Shore to create a circle-island road. One look at the arduous cliffs, and you'll see why.

Backtrack your way down to Highway 50 and go northwest along the beach-rimmed highway, where you'll spot the Pacific Missile Range military compound, with its **BARKING SANDS BEACH**, named after the sound the sand supposedly makes when the wind hits it just right. A little further up is the *makai* (ocean side) turn-off for **POLIHALE BEACH**. A dirt road leads you through sugar cane fields to one of the most stunning beaches in the state. This remote, amazing length of sand and dunes is bordered on one end by rugged sea cliffs. Almost always sunny and empty, this is the beach you've always dreamt about. But avoid swimming when the water is turbulent: There are no hunky lifeguards to save you here!

OVERVIEW OF THE SCENE AND SCENESTERS

Kauai is what a lot of people fantasize about when they think of Hawaii. It's full of huge, empty beaches, lush river valleys, exotic rainforests, jagged cliffs with long thin waterfalls, and an overall primordial feeling—basically your postcard Hollywood version of Paradise. Come to think of it, Hollywood has exploited the place a little! *South Pacific, Jurassic Park, King Kong, Blue Hawaii, 10, Hook, Outbreak*, and the artistic cinematic triumph *Throw Mama from the Train* (!) were all shot here, as well as lots of TV shows. So you probably have seen Kauai, you just never knew it. Now is your chance to see it for real, without a Hollywood filter. Sure, Kauai may be smaller and quieter than the other neighbor islands, but that's just the way people like it—Kauai usually ranks as the number one favorite Hawaiian island on travelers' lists.

Tourism on Kauai tends to be less flashy and more eco-friendly than on Oahu and Maui. More emphasis is put on the dramatic outdoors and slower lifestyle, rather than mega-resorts. Having said that, the areas of Poipu in the south, Kapaa on the eastern coast, and Princeville in the north feel like the tourist magnets they are. Most of Kauai's queer community lives north of the Wailua River, especially up along Highway 580 in the Wailua Homesteads, and a few gay bed and breakfasts are found around here as well. Gays and lesbians are extremely well organized and cohesive on Kauai compared to the other islands, with frequent potlucks, movie nights at people's homes, and bonfires at Kealia Beach, which visitors are more than welcome to join (fresh faces always needed). It has been said that on any given holiday the gay crowd is putting on some kind of well-attended event.

There is no totally gay bar on Kauai, but Secret Beach and Larsen's Beach (near what used to be the main gay nude area called Donkey Beach) attract a gathering of gays, but nudity in Kauai can incur fines, so be warned. The gay group Lambda Aloha sponsors a weekly Friday-night LGBT beach bonfire (*See To Do and See*) and is politically active. Be sure to check Lambda Aloha's info number (808/823-MAHU) for upcoming events before you get to the island. Malama Pono, the Kauai AIDS agency, also sponsors a lot of island activities.

TO DO AND SEE

ALEXANDER DAY SPA AND SALON A gay-owned pampering facility located at the Kauai Marriott Resort in Lihue, Alexander offers massage, facials, nail services, waxing, hair care, and even bridal styling. Alexander has 25 years of experience in Beverly Hills working on celebs like Demi Moore, Heather Locklear, President Ford, and even Roseanne. Specialized treatments include Hawaiian sea salt, full body microdermabrasion and advanced Hawaiian lomilomi techniques with special herbs from the islands. 3610 Rice Street, Lihue. (866) 932-9772, (808) 246-4918. AlexanderSpa.com

FRIDAY NIGHT LGBT COMMUNITY BONFIRE This weekly get-together at Kealia Beach is *the* thing for the traveling homo to do on Kauai. Men and women come to roast weenies (bring your own hot dog and drinks, buns supplied!), "talk story," and hobnob Hawaiian-style—everyone is welcome. Sometimes there is a small handful of people, and sometimes nearly a whole town shows up. Use the exit (opening in the guard rail) just north of the 10-mile marker on the highway. Call (808) 823-MAHU for more info, LAMBDAALOHA.COM/EVENTS/COMMUNITYBONFIRE.HTML

LILO KAUAI CRUISES There are a number of sea tours up the Na Pali Coast—from kayaking to sailing charters—but why not go with a native Hawaiian? Liko Hookano was born and raised on Kauai, and his family comes from the "Forbidden Island" of Niihau. Lilo takes just 24 passengers on his 49-foot power catamaran out of Kikiaola small boat harbor (the closest harbor to the Na Pali Coast) to explore sea caves, cascading waterfalls, uninhabited lush valleys, pods of humpback whales and dolphins, and miles of white sand beaches, providing snorkeling gear, lunch, and best of all, an authentic commentary on island lore, culture, history, and funny true stories. (888) 732-5456, (808) 338-0333. LIKO-KAUAI.COM

NIGHTLIFE

TAHITI NUI For a funky, home-grown look into the Hawaii of yesteryear, the Tahiti Nui in Hanalei is the real thing. This bar/restaurant caters to the locals with no pretense, and it was the first watering hole to open up on the north shore over 40 years ago. Local Hawaiian bands belt it out, hula dancers get up and do impromptu shows at the drop of a hat, and the porch features great views. The fresh fish is prepared Tahitian-style, but really go for the very local scene (not to mention the lethal mai tais). The crowd is very straight and at times a bit rough, so don't expect to be too "out" here. But it's fun and friendly nonetheless. 5-5134 Kuhio Highway, Hanalei. (808) 826-6277

TRADEWINDS BAR Although Kauai has no gay bar, Tradewinds, "A South Seas Bar" in the Coconut Marketplace since 1979, is popular with local gays and lesbians. Its casual, open-air, party-hearty atmosphere includes video games, darts, karaoke, DJs, live local bands, dancing, and Sunday night satellite football. Be sure to order a 24-ounce Big Ass Draft—the take home glass needs to be seen to be believed! 484 Kuhio Highway, Kapaa. (808) 822-1621. TRADEWINDS-KAUAI.COM

LODGING (LGBT)

ANUENUE PLANTATION BED & BREAKFAST This modern five-acre estate away from the noise of traffic and surf is owned by Harry and Fred who offer two spiffy, comfortable guest rooms in their tasteful home. A separate cottage also resides on the property, and every room has wide-open panoramas of the sky and ocean and mountains, including a perfect shot of the world's wettest, Mount Waialeale. There's a guest lounge/library, and wellness and human growth seminars, music, and dances frequently occur in the windowed ballroom. P.O. Box 226, Kapaa. (888) 371-7716, (808) 823-8335. ANUENUE.COM **INEXPENSIVE**

MAHINA KAI OCEAN VILLA This straight-friendly B&B is still one of the gayest on the island, housed in a blue-tiled Asian-Pacific house. Its name means "moon over the water." You can sip tea around a gorgeous Oriental koi pond atrium, or bask naked by the outdoor lagoon swimming pool or eight-man hot tub surrounded by elegant Japanese gardens. The two-acre property also includes banyan trees and Royal Hawaiian palms. Personal paintings and art adorn the three Japanese-inspired rooms, complete with shoji sliding doors, and there's also a separate two-bedroom apartment. Mahina Kai opened its doors in 1985 as an exclusively gay B&B, and it's still gay owned by friendly chaps Joe & Rob. P.O. Box 699, Anahola. (800) 337-1134, (808) 822-9451. MAHINAKAI.COM **MODERATE, NUDIST-FRIENDLY**

MOHALA KE OLA This serene, gay-owned guest retreat has four reasonably-priced private rooms, and plenty of peace and quiet from the surrounding state forest. Awesome mountain and waterfall views encircle the pool, hot tub, and sunbathing deck, and be sure to take advantage of the onsite lomilomi Hawaiian massage, Reiki, or acupuncture. Hiking to Secret Falls and Sleeping Giant is possible from the house, and kayak and bicycle rental is offered too. A tropical breakfast is served by the warm and friendly owner, Ed, who offers you his knowledge of the island and environment. 5663 Ohelo Road, Kapaa. (888) GO-KAUAI, (808) 823-6398. WATERFALLBNB.COM **INEXPENSIVE**

LODGING (MAINSTREAM)

GRAND HYATT KAUAI RESORT AND SPA Indeed, this is one of Hawaii's grandest and highest-ranked hotels fronting a great beach on the southern shore of the island. Located on over 50 acres, the resort's rooms are large (nearly 600 sq. ft.) with marble bathrooms and spacious private lanais or balconies, and there are several pools and hot tubs, five acres of saltwater swimming lagoons and a man-made beach, four tennis courts, one of the best fitness centers on the island, and a 25,000-sq.-ft. ANARA Spa with lava-rock shower gardens and indoor/outdoor treatment rooms. Even with all these superlatives, the place does not feel over-the-top, but casually elegant with its 1920s-style island architecture. 1571 Poipu Road, Poipu. (808) 742-1234. KAUAI.HYATT.COM **EXPENSIVE, KID-FRIENDLY, HANDICAP-FRIENDLY**

PRINCEVILLE RESORT Originally dubbed "the prison" by locals who weren't thrilled at the first dark and inward structure, the Princeville Resort was completely gutted and renovated in 1991 at something close to a $100 million. The hotel holds the plum spot on Kauai's North Shore, with each of the 252 rooms looking on to an immense and perfect view of Hanalei Bay. Although the weather is a bit unreliable, the spectacular setting and a Robert Trent Jones, Jr. golf course along immaculate bluffs overlooking the ocean, make up for it, not to mention the resort's posh furniture, fountains, statues, and marble floors. 5520 Kahaku Road, Hanalei. (866) 716-8100, (808) 826-9644. PRINCEVILLEHOTELHAWAII.COM **EXPENSIVE, KID-FRIENDLY, HANDICAP-FRIENDLY**

WAIMEA PLANTATION COTTAGES One of the most unique and authentic places to stay on Hawaii, these secluded beachfront cottages set in a peaceful coconut grove were built in the early 1900s for sugar plantation employees. Each cottage has been thoroughly modernized and refurbished, but still retains a historical air about them with period furnishings of mahogany, rattan, or wicker and a front porch overlooking a wide, grassy lawn. Body wraps, body scrubs, facials, acupuncture, and yoga are available in their onsite spa, and there's a beachside pool and nearby black sand beach. 9400 Kaumualii Highway, Waimea. (877) 997-6667, (808) 338-1625. WAIMEA-PLANTATION.COM **EXPENSIVE, KID-FRIENDLY**

DINING

CAFFE COCO Calling itself an art gallery/espresso bar/café this eatery is housed within a restored wooden plantation home with a lime green storefront, rattan furniture, local art on the walls, outside garden seating with nightly music, and a tin roof. Breakfast (turkey sausage omelet), lunch (Thai noodle salad with peanut dressing), and dinner (spinach fettuccine with ahi and roasted tomatoes) are all made with fresh local produce, and every dish tastes gourmet, but at good prices. Also offered are daily tastings of their homemade jams and salsa. 4-369 Kuhio Highway, Wailua. (808) 822-7990 **MODERATE**

GAYLORD'S Located within the grand Kilohana Plantation Tudor mansion (now transformed into an upscale artsy shopping complex), this restaurant's courtyard vistas look over the sprawling lawns, creating a plantation ambience. Named after a member of the prominent Wilcox family, the menu offers dishes like herb-crusted rack of lamb and Australian flame-broiled filet mignon. Gorgeous setting and tasty food. 3-2087 Kaumualii Highway, Lihue. (808) 245-9593. GAYLORDSKAUAI.COM **EXPENSIVE**

PLANTATION GARDENS One of the most atmospheric spots to eat on Kauai, enjoy classic plantation-era fine dining on the lanai of an historic 1930s manor house that belonged to the manager of Hawaii's first sugar plantation at Poipu beach. Overlook lush gardens filled with all kinds of plant life while you try locally-grown fresh organic vegetables and herbs as well as fish, seafood, and meats grilled over kiawe, a native mesquite wood. 2253 Poipu Road, Koloa. (808) 742-2121. PGRESTAURANT.COM **EXPENSIVE**

HAWAII

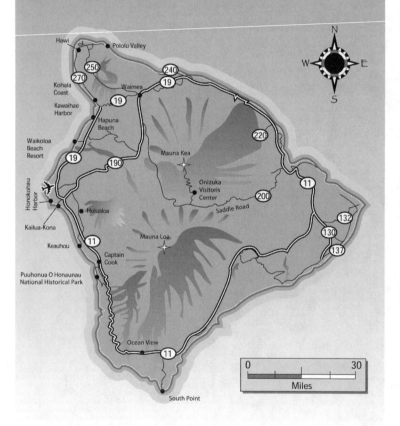

Hawi
Pololu Valley
250
270
240
19
Kohala Coast
Waimea
19
Kawaihae Harbor
Hapuna Beach
220
Waikoloa Beach Resort
Mauna Kea
19
190
Onizuka Visitoris Center
200
11
Honokohau Harbor
Saddle Road
132
Holualoa
130
Kailua-Kona
Mauna Loa
137
Keauhou
11
Captain Cook
Puuhonua O Honaunau National Historical Park

Ocean View
11

South Point

N
W   E
S

0   30
Miles

ISLAND FACTS

HAWAII IS NICKNAMED: "The Orchid Isle" and more generally called "The Big Island"

ISLAND COLOR: Red

ISLAND FLOWER: Lehua

LAND MASS: 4,028 sq. miles/1,047 sq. km (and growing!)

POPULATION: 171,000 est.

HIGHEST POINT: Mauna Kea at 13,796 feet/4,205 m

RAINFALL: 25 inches/64 cm in Kailua, 145 inches/368 cm in Hilo

OUT TRAVELER RATINGS GUIDE

GAY-FRIENDLY: ▼▼

GAY SCENE: ▼▼

LESBIAN SCENE: ▼▼

PRO-GAY LAWS: ▼▼▼

HIV RESOURCES: ▼▼▼▼

The island of Hawaii is the youngest of the major islands, and the largest island in the U.S. It is home to the longest continual volcanic eruption in human history at Kilauea (since 1983). It also has the largest mountain mass in the world, Mauna Kea, measured at over 31,000 feet from its base 18,000 feet underwater. The island was birthplace of King Kamehameha in Kohala in 1758, and the famous British explorer Captain Cook was killed here in 1779.

GEOGRAPHICAL OVERVIEW

Flights to Kona land at the Keahole Airport, in the middle of a huge, barren, black lava field bordering the runway. But heading south on Highway 19 from the airport, civilization quickly pops up when you turn toward the ocean at Palani Road and into the heart of **KAILUA–KONA VILLAGE**. The town had only one stoplight up through the 1980s. Now it is a major boomtown, with traffic and shopping malls to prove it. But fishermesn still stand solemn on the seawall in town for hours, aunties yawn and sell flower leis on the sidewalk, and kids scream and jump off the pier, just like in the old days.

The pier in front of the **KING KAMEHAMEHA BEACH HOTEL** along Alii Drive is where diving, snorkeling, parasailing, and other cruises take off from. A little beach in front of the hotel offers the only real sand in town. You will also spot the reconstructed **AHUENA HEIAU** here, near where King Kamehameha spent the last years of his life. Just down the street is the **FIRST CHRISTIAN CHURCH** in the islands (made from coral stone and koa wood) and across the street from the church is the fascinating **HULIHEE PALACE**, where the Hawaiian royalty spent their holidays. It's now open to the public. The little shopping village includes the historic **KONA INN** (where Errol Flynn and Tyrone Power used to come for holidays).

If you continue south on the coastal **ALII DRIVE,** it will lead past condos and homes to the **KAHALUU BEACH PARK**. There isn't much of a beach here, but plenty of friendly turtles and fish to snorkel among.

If you keep heading south on Highway 11, the **QUEEN KAAHUMANU HIGHWAY** begins to ascend to nearly 1,000 feet as it enters Kona coffee country and small roadside towns. Keep your eyes peeled for **NAPOOPOO ROAD** on the ocean side of the highway after the 111 mile marker. Follow this winding road to the remarkable **KEALAKEKUA BAY**. Renowned as the spot where Captain Cook was killed, a small obelisk stands in his honor on the opposite side of the bay under the cliffs, near where large snorkeling boats come to dump tourists into the crystal water. Spinner dolphins often visit the bay, circling the astonished kayakers and snorkelers.

Keep heading south on the coastal road of Highay 160 out of Kealakekua Bay, and you'll soon hit the stunning and sacred **PUUHONUA O HONAUNAU NATIONAL PARK**. Explore the centuries-old ruins of huge temples and 15-foot walls the Hawaiians built as a sanctuary for refugees of wars and *kapu* law-breakers. Kahuna priests here would exonerate the offenders of their official sins through rituals.

From the park, keep on Highway 160 as it snakes back up to Highway 11, and follow the signs to **ST. BENEDICT'S PAINTED CHURCH**. Stop by this genuine little church to behold the interior painted with trees and murals and stars on the ceiling, by the artistically inclined Father John Velge around the turn of the century. It stirs the soul of even the most atheistic.

Keeping on Highway 11 further south, the road becomes more and more twisted and the population thins out a bit. You will pass through the largest macadamia nut orchards in the state before you hit **HAWAIIAN OCEAN VIEW ESTATES**, or for those in the

HAWAII The Big Island-Kona

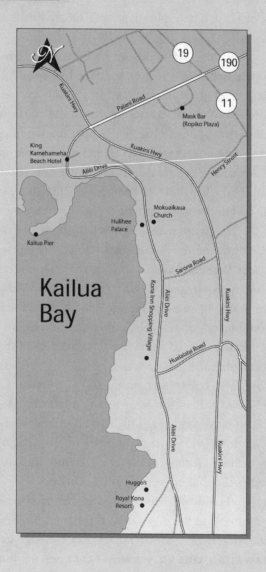

19

190

11

Kuakini Hwy

Palani Road

Mask Bar
(Kopiko Plaza)

Kuakini Hwy

King
Kamehameha
Beach Hotel

Aliëi Drive

Henry Street

Mokuaikaua
Church

Hulihee
Palace

Kailua Pier

Sarona Road

Kailua
Bay

Kona Inn Shopping Village

Aliëi Drive

Kuakini Hwy

Hualalalai Road

Aliëi Drive

Kuakini Hwy

Huggo's

Royal Kona
Resort

know, "Hove." Touting itself as the world's largest subdivision, this "neighborhood" stretches so far back up the banks of Mauna Loa that it nearly snows at the end of it. Everyone from millionaires to food stamp recipients (and many gays and lesbians at both ends of the spectrum) seem to own a chunk of the lava back here. Further on you'll pass South Point and be on your way to Hilo.

If you instead head north out of Kailua-Kona town on Highway 19, you will find the sign for the **HONOKOHAU HARBOR** on your left. This is the site of Kona's gay-popular beach, as well as home to sports fishing charters. The desert-like **KOHALA COAST** stretches north from here. This is where a majority of the most out-of-control luxurious resorts in the state reside amid the stark lava rock. The show-stopper of them all is at the first turn-off you hit, near the 76 mile marker, called the **WAIKOLOA RESORT AREA**. Included here are two excellent golf courses, a nice beach (Anaehoomalu Bay), some classy resorts, and the amazingly opulent **HILTON WAIKOLOA VILLAGE** (see Lodging).

Further north are more resorts lined up along the coast, including the **MAUNA LANI** and its famous golf course. The best beach on an island not known for its beaches is **HAPUNA STATE BEACH**, near the 69 mile marker. Smooth white sand with an absence of rocks and coral makes for a postcard-perfect swimming and boogie boarding.

At the junctions of 19 and 270, be sure to take a peek at the **PUUKOHOLA HEIAU**. It was built to the war god Kukailimoku after a kahuna priest prophesied that King Kamehameha would subdue all the Hawaiian Islands upon its completion, which of course he went ahead and did. It is also said to be the last Hawaiian temple where routine human sacrifices were carried out (not pretty virgins but ugly slaves). Head up on Highway 270 past Kawaihae Harbor up toward Hawi along the dramatic, Spartan desert coast that looks like it was shipped in from Baja California. The scenery quickly turns green as you near the village of **HAWI**. Stop here and snoop the artsy little shops and galleries.

Further past Hawi is Kapaau, where the nearly seven foot tall **KING KAMEHAMEHA STATUE** stands, which is actually life size! At the very end of Highway 270 is the lookout to the lush, remote **POLOLU VALLEY**.

From Hawi you can loop south on Highway 250 on the green rolling hills of the **KOHALA MOUNTAIN RANGE**, which is frequently rainbowed. The cheerful road descends into the ranching town of **WAIMEA**. In this *paniolo* (cowboy) village it looks like Marlboro Man would be at home, albeit with shorts and sandals on. Headquarters of the 225,000-acre **PARKER RANCH**, you can visit the Parker family home, **PUOPELU**, off Highway 190 south of town, last owned by queer rancher Richard Smart (see sidebar).

If you continued south on Highway 190, you would encounter the turn-off for **SADDLE ROAD**. There's not a heck of a lot to see up here except close-up and overwhelming views of **MAUNA KEA**

HAWAII The Big Island-Hilo

and **MAUNA LOA** mountains, which are dusted with snow in the winter. Saddle Road crosses the island and ends in Hilo.

The **ONIZUKA VISITOR'S CENTER** is up about 9,000 feet on the slopes of Mauna Kea, and is named after the Big Island astronaut who perished in the Challenger disaster. If you have a four-wheel drive and a lot of guts, take the ragged dirt road up to the windswept, chilly summit for a splendid sunset. Since it is above 40% of the earth's atmosphere and far from continental dust, the surrealistic summit of Mauna Kea is home to the world's most powerful land-based telescopes (none open to the public).

If you keep on Saddle Road, it drops you off in the **DOWNTOWN AREA OF HILO**, which still has the feel of an old sugar plantation town, despite refurbishments. Storefronts dating back to the 1910s line the main drag of **KAMEHAMEHA AVENUE**, overlooking the highway and bayfront. Walk up **WAIANUENUE ROAD** and you will pass the most dramatic building in town: a lavish two-story post office with white columns and an outdoor courtyard. Across the street is **KALAKAUA PARK**, with a statue of the Merrie Monarch, an impressive banyan tree, and antique buildings lining the south edge.

If you drive up for another mile or so on Waianuenue, you'll come across the turn-off for **RAINBOW FALLS**, a postcard perfect waterfall in the back of the town. King Kamehameha is said to have buried the bones of his father in a cave below the falls.

Back in town, on Haili Street lies the **LYMAN MUSEUM**. Treat yourself to a succinct lesson in Hawaiian history with poi pounders, feathered cloaks, Korean dresses, and Hawaiian Bibles. Upstairs is one of the most incredible rock collections you have ever laid eyes on. Visit the **LYMAN HOUSE** next door, lovingly built by a die-hard missionary family.

Heading back down Haili Street to the bay front, you will pass the grand, remodeled 1925 **PALACE THEATER**, home to artsy movies, live concerts, and plays. Nearby on Kamehameha is the **PACIFIC TSUNAMI MUSEUM**, which documents the tragedies of the 1946 and 1960 tsunamis that devastated Hilo's populace and wiped out huge parts of the town. Then walk right along the stores on the bay front until you reach some blue tarps at the intersection of Mamo and Kamehameha. You are now at the best **FARMER'S MARKET** on the whole island. Purchase fresh white pineapples, jackfruit, papayas, organic bananas, flowers, nuts, fish, as well as plants and clothing. Although Saturday is the big morning, there's usually someone there any day of the week hawking their wares.

Continue on Kamehameha over a bridge and you'll see the **SUISAN FISH AUCTION MARKET** on the ocean side of the road. The catch of the day is thrown out onto the decks for the hungry buyers in the morning, and it smells like it. Take a walk around **BANYAN DRIVE**, dripping with huge cavernous trees, with the pretty Coconut Island as a backdrop—a favorite spot for fishermen and family picnics. The nearby 30 acre **LILIUOKALANI GARDENS**, complete with Japanese pagodas, arch bridges, and stone lanterns, makes a nice shot for the honeymoon album. Hilo's small handful of hotels is along Banyan Drive, including the **HAWAII NANILOA AND HILO SEASIDE**.

Carry on past Banyan Drive and drive to Kalanianaole Avenue and the best beaches around Hilo. The term beach is used loosely here, since there is usually no sand, but lagoons with swimming and snorkeling. At the dead end of Kalanianaole Avenue, you may find homos at the far side of **RICHARDSON'S BEACH**.

Heading north on **HIGHWAY 19** from Hilo, you'll pass some large ravines caused by the run-off from Mauna Kea, and some small villages. Keep an eye out on the ocean side of the road for the four mile scenic coastal route (past the 7 mile marker), and you'll come upon the **HAWAII TROPICAL BOTANICAL GARDENS**, with over 2,000 exotic species that makes an attractive stop.

Back on the main highway, you will see the turn-off for the **AKAKA FALLS STATE PARK** between the 13 and 14 mile markers. Stroll along a nature trail with bamboo groves and lush foliage until you get to an easy lookout at the stunning 440–foot drop waterfall slinking its way down a sheer cliff wall.

Back on Highway 19, you will snake up the Hamakua Coast's dense rainforest ravines and rich fields of abandoned sugar cane. Turn on Highway 240 and go through the old sugar town of **HONOKAA**, and then on to the lookout for the **WAIPIO VALLEY**, one of the wonders of the Big Island. A huge open valley with high green walls greets the eye like something out of a dream. Taro is still cultivated on the ancient land as it has been for centuries,

**CATTLE NEAR HALEAKALA CRATER,
THE WORLD'S LARGEST DORMANT VOLCANO**

THE BIG ISLAND'S QUEER RANCHER

Richard Smart stands as one of the better-known gays in recent Hawaiian history. Smart was directly descended from John Palmer Parker, who jumped ship in Hawaii as a teenager in 1809, made friends with King Kamehameha, married his granddaughter, and ended up owning what at one point was the largest individually-owned ranch in the U.S.A. with well over 500,000 acres (it still covers about 10% of the island). As an infant, Richard Smart became sole heir to this wealthy Parker Ranch in Waimea after his mother died of tuberculosis in the early 1900s.

The ranch was run by trustees until 1960s, when the flamboyant Richard, fresh from a successful run as an actor and singer on Broadway and in Paris, took over the estate. His love of the theater and lavish demeanor (not to mention his artsy friends) raised a few of the old-time *paniolo* cowboys' eyebrows on the ranch, but everyone eventually abided. Smart added an impressive art collection to his family's Puopelu Home, with work by Pissaro, Monet, and Kluge, and opened the Kahilu Theater in Waimea, named after his mother Thelma. His philanthropy made the town into the

and horseback and carriage tours can take you down in the valley, which was once a huge ancient Hawaiian settlement.

Making your way back down the coast to Hilo again, if you instead head south out of Hilo town you'd be on Highway 11. The turn–off for Highway 130 will take you into the heart of the PUNA district. This alternative, hippy refuge region is where a large

THE BIG ISLAND'S QUEER RANCHER

arts center that it still is today.

Richard Smart died in 1992, and as soon as the bucket was kicked, his two sons (from his one "marriage") became involved in a fierce lawsuit dispute over the inheritance of the estate. All was settled, and now Parker Ranch is peacefully owned by the Parker Ranch Foundation Trust, which helps fund Waimea education, arts, and medical institutions. It's the first time in six generations that it has no single individual ownership.

Visitors can still visit the Puopelu family home, off Highway 190 near Waimea (808/885-5433). The family's Impressionist and Chinese art, statues, and antiques still adorn the scenic 1862 home, which sports a French Provincial interior, and a yellow Hawaiian Victorian exterior. Of course, the guides don't mention the fact that Richard was gay, or that he's buried in the mausoleum out back, next to his last boyfriend. Don't forget to pick up your cassette copy of Richard Smart singing the best of Broadway, available at the gift counter.

chunk of the state's biggest illegal cash crop, *pakalolo*, is grown in the rich and wet landscape. Government helicopters have been flying overhead for years, trying to shut down local production of the sweet-smelling illegal herb. Most of the gay and lesbian populace on the Hilo side of the island lives in and around the Puna district.

PAHOA is the very funky center of Puna that has wooden

THE WORLD'S LARGEST SPANDEX CONVENTION

For those of you who can't wait until summer for a good ogle at all the guys in cute little swimming briefs and spandex, The Ironman Triathlon (IronmanLive.com) is the ultimate experience. Kailua–Kona town comes alive with thousands of extra visitors and competitors filling the streets from all over the world—something like the United Nations of Speedos. Up to a month before the actual Ironman date, you will notice swarms of dudes and dudettes exercising up and down the coast, frantically trying to acclimatize to Kona's hot, harsh terrain. On the third Saturday in October, get up early to watch the guys and gals take off from the Kona Pier just after dawn, swim 2.4 miles, mount their bikes for the 112 mile round trip ride to Hawi, then race 26.2 miles down to the finish line set up at the Kailua pier. Hundreds of visitors and residents alike cheer on the Ironpeople every step of the way, with aid stations set up all over the course.

sidewalks and old Western storefronts, and where earth mothers and moonbeams congregate to "talk story." Also, check out the old-fashioned **AKEBONO THEATER** (the oldest in Hawaii since 1919).

Driving out of Pahoa south on 130, you'll pass the steam vents about 3.5 miles later that are gay-popular (*see To See and Do*). Highway 130 abruptly ends at some recent **LAVA FLOWS** covering the pavement. The road used to continue from here along the coast to the Volcanoes National Park, until lava flows from eruptions in the 1980s and 1990s put an end to that. It's at this end of 130

THE WORLD'S LARGEST SPANDEX CONVENTION

Driving around the Kona Coast that day is complicated, with lots of detours, so stay put at your hotel or in town for convenience. By mid-afternoon, the quickest athletes are past the finish line and into the arms of the waiting medics and massage practitioners. You will be amazed at the Ironmen who are missing limbs or race in wheelchairs who finish quite early! (Bound to make the buffest of you feel out of shape.)

Of note: in 1996, Jim Howley was the first person to do the Ironman as a publicly disclosed HIV-positive person. Diagnosed with the virus in the early 1980s and with full-blown AIDS in 1989, he took on the Ironman as a way to "defy death." At 35, Jim beat out many other competitors in the field. The West Hawaii AIDS Foundation proudly set up a refueling station to support him and all the other non-disclosed HIV-positive people in the race.

where you may be able to take the long, multiple-mile hike to the present lava flows, depending on the course of the current eruption (sometimes the lava is closer to the national park end of the road). Although the park service shakes their tsk tsk finger at the danger of it, many people hike across the crackling new lava to catch an up-close glimpse of the lava rivers emptying into the ocean. Of course a few of those hikers are no longer with us!

Follow the coastal Highway 137 until the road ends again at **KALAPANA**. Here, almost 200 homes were slowly destroyed by encroaching lava. You may be able to stand on top of the black lava rock and see the huge steam clouds from the lava flows hitting the sea in the far distance.

From the Kalapana dead end, if you turn around and head north on Highway 137 along the coast, you will go over a series of dips until you pass the gay-popular **KEHENA BLACK SAND BEACH**. The gay-managed **KALANI OCEANSIDE RETREAT** is just a short ways up from that (*see Lodging*). The lush and quiet Highway 137 is called Red Road, and if followed further will take you past the Ahalanui Park and its warm soaking pond along the ocean. The water hovers above 90 degrees and there are usually not too many people, except on weekends.

After your adventure in funky Puna, head back to the main circle-island Highway 11 going south, and along the roadside you will spot a few **ORCHID NURSERIES**, most open for walking tours, since this is the major orchid growing region in the U.S. In fact, keep an eye out for species growing on the side of the road like weeds.

A few more miles and you are at the entrance of the **HAWAII VOLCANOES NATIONAL PARK**. This is the main tourist draw for the whole island, and deservedly not to be missed. Most of the action centers around the **CRATER RIM DRIVE**, with its older non-lava vents. When you pull into the park, the first thing you will hit is the Visitor's Center. Stop in for the latest viewing info posted on the wall, plus a cool 20 minute film of past eruptions wrecking mayhem.

Across the street is the **VOLCANO HOUSE** (*see Lodging*), rebuilt from the original 1800s structure. Further on Crater Rim Drive you'll hit the **JAGGER MUSEUM**, with seismographs, displays of lava-eaten boots, and a colorful mural explaining the different Hawaiian gods and goddesses, fire goddess Pele undoubtedly being the local star.

Further along the drive, you will cross incredibly stark lavascapes, some as recent as the '70s. They appear as mammoth rock brownies of varying shades stretching off into the distance. Stop and walk to the edge of **HALEMAUMAU CRATER**, the traditional home of Pele, and peer into a huge pit that was alive and bubbling for a good part of the 19th century. It still holds a quiet power to it.

The next turn–off will be at the **CHAIN OF CRATERS ROAD** to your right, heading toward the ocean. Depending on the lava activity, it may or may not be worth the 45 minute drive to the coast to witness distant steam clouds produced from the hot lava entering the ocean. The biggest action actually takes place at the **PUU OO VENT**, about eight miles east of the Crater Rim Drive, up on the mountainside. Periodic lava spouts have reached up to 2,000 feet, and you may see red glows in the evening depending on what Pele's up to. If you have the time, by all means fly over it via aircraft from the Hilo Airport. The sight of red liquid rock burping and spurting and cascading is nothing less than spiritually fantastic.

South of the national park is a straight-away stretch of Highway 11 along the vast flanks of Mauna Loa, one of the most remote regions on the island. Don't forget to pull into the **PUNALUU BEACH PARK** which, if you're lucky, will have some large hawksbill turtles on its shores (it's a major nesting site). Head further south on 11, and you will ultimately hit one of the prettiest towns on the island, the old sugar village of **NAALEHU**. Be sure to check out the massive tree on the side of the road that Mark Twain planted way back when.

Past Naalehu is the *makai* (ocean side) turn for **SOUTH POINT**, the southernmost point in the U.S., about the latitude of Mexico City. Twelve miles of undeveloped road and an army of steel windmills later, you are standing on the edge of dramatically windswept cliffs. If you take the easternmost fork of South Point road, it will end at a boat ramp area where you can park and walk a coastal dirt road north to **GREEN SANDS BEACH**. Be prepared for a windy hour-long stroll that will take you to a desert-like cove with a small olive colored beach. It's made from the semi-precious olivine, a by-product of the lava hitting the sea. Only in Hawaii can you get red, black, white, and green sand in your swimsuit!

OVERVIEW OF THE SCENE AND SCENESTERS

The Big Island is just that—big—and in some ways is treated by residents as two separate islands. The western Kona side is dry, sunny, and touristy, the eastern Hilo side is wet, lush, and very local. Everyone has their preferred area of the island, and argue about the pros and cons of each to no end.

The wide, arid expanses and huge ranches of North Kona can make you feel like you are in any Western state (despite the palm trees). The Kohala Coast north of Kailua-Kona town, home to many monolithic resorts and black lava fields, is said to be the sunniest part of the whole state. The impressive slopes of the volcanoes of Mauna Kea, Mauna Loa, and Hualalai are all easily visible along this coast, and you can meander up Saddle Road that traverses the island to get a closer look at them. Kona overall has a well-oiled tourist infrastructure, lots of excellent diving (with manta rays no less), snorkeling, whale watching, horseback riding, golf, sports fishing, and kayaking.

Since so much of the state's history is linked to the Big Island, Kona is also home to some of the largest, best preserved *heiau* (Hawaiian temples) and petroglyph fields (ancient rock carvings) in Hawaii. The **PUUHONUA O HONAUNAU** (Place of Refuge) is an awesome ancient sacred site, located in the greener region of rural South Kona, where the famous Kona coffee is grown and roasted.

There's a lot of driving involved to get around, but be sure to spend enough time to explore all the differences around the island.

Day activities are plentiful while the nightlife is pretty much dead on arrival, although Kona is home to the only true gay bar outside of Honolulu. Regardless, the gay male community on the Kona side is a bit hidden, while the women's scene is alive, with well-organized get togethers listed in the Lesbian Brunch Bulletin. Kona offers a nice selection of gay and lesbian B&Bs, many congregated south around the Honaunau area.

Hilo acts as the exact opposite of Kona. It rains here more than anywhere in the state except Kauai. Don't be surprised if it is cloudy and gray during your entire time in Hilo. If you ask a resident they will say the rain and drizzle and deluge (what they refer to as "liquid sunshine") isn't that bad at all—in fact they wouldn't have it any other way. Given the old, colorful, rainforest feel of this side of the island, you'll understand what they mean.

Hilo is undiluted by tourism, keeping its distinct flavor and character of a proud Hawaiian town. The Puna area, with its black sand beaches and steam vents and rich foliage, is as organic as the island chain gets. And don't forget, the volcano goddess Pele resides on this side of the island, and you can fly over her turbulent furnace in the Hawaii Volcanoes National Park by helicopter or airplane.

Hilo's gay community is not really centered in Hilo town, but south in the fundamentally bohemian Puna district, where a chunk of the LGBT B&Bs can be found. Here the gay community is tight knit, with queers coming out of the rural woodwork for miles to enjoy the large parties at people's homes.

The black sand nude beach at Kehena is quite social, and there are various community events sponsored by the local AIDS organization. The gay-owned Kalani Resort near Kehena also puts on a number of queer get-togethers throughout the year, including nude men's weeks and Body Electric massage workshops. The women's community is well-organized here as well, with several women's guesthouses.

TO SEE AND DO

BLUE HAWAIIAN HELICOPTERS With one of the best safety records in the state, Blue Hawaiian is seen as the premier helicopter company in Hawaii. They leave from both sides of the island on a number of short and long tours that dip into uninhabited valleys and remote parts of the island you'd never see otherwise, but the real showstopper are the flights from Hilo that go directly over the active volcano vent in the Volcanoes National Park. You are given comfy headphones and a fascinating narration by the pilot, and everyone gets a window seat and video of the flight. The Big Island is one of the only places in the world where you can fly over an active lava vent, and it's not to be missed. (800) 745-BLUE, (808) 961-5600, BLUEHAWAIIAN.COM

HAWAII HEALING OHANA The spa and healing center is run by a long-time island gay couple, and it's Kailua-Kona's largest and winner of numerous awards. They are also the exclusive manufacturers of their own brand and line of all-natural body and bath products. Their special onsite treatments include an infrared sauna, aroma steambath, coconut sugar body wrap, Hawaiian hot stone massages, reflexology, certified organic cleansing programs, and medical massage. 75-5799 Alii Drive, Suite A3, Kailua-Kona, (808) 331-1050, HAWAIIHEALINGOHANA.COM

KONA HONU MANTA RAY NIGHT SNORKEL OR DIVE Kona's Keauhou Bay is one of the best places on earth to swim up close to harmless manta rays, an elegant nocturnal beast that feeds on plankton. Kona Honu Divers shine huge floodlights onto the rays (some with 12-foot wing spans) to attract their dinner, and divers or snorkelers can swim among the rays as they do a kind of underwater ballet. It's called one of the most unique ocean experiences in the world. (888) 333-4668, KONAHONUDIVERS.COM

PAHOA STEAM VENTS The natural steam vents off of Highway 130, past Pahoa at mile marker 15, are a hike *makai* (toward the ocean) from the scenic lookout pull-over on the road, and only for the adventurous. Formed by sulfur exhaust compliments of Madame Pele, these vents amid the foliage range from a small crawl-through cavern, to bowl-like structures you can climb down into, to one-man, open-air sitting chambers. The steam is usually at the right temperature to enjoy a nice sweat. Popular with residents who normally use them nude, there's a following of gay users too. The protocol is to keep quiet and not disturb the other users in their respective vents. (The trail does get muddy, and there are no public facilities.) It's a truly Hawaiian experience.

NIGHTLIFE

CAPTAIN BEAN'S DINNER CRUISE This unabashed booze cruise on a 150–foot mock Hawaiian vessel is worth it for its camp value alone, with non-straight acting, loincloth-clad guys dancing right on top of your table, as well as straight male tourists being forced to don grass skirts and wigs! A decent Polynesian-style meal is served, booze is included, and the Conga line they save 'til the very last. It's a fun way to get out onto the ocean and let your hair down, and it's nearly the wildest Kona nightlife ever really gets! 73-4800 Kanalani Street, Kailua–Kona. (866) 898-2519, (808) 329-2955. ROBERTSHAWAII.COM

MASK The only official gay bar outside of Honolulu, Mask is in a strip mall near downtown Kailua–Kona. It is tiny but clean, with the ever-present Karaoke mike and a horseshoe shaped bar. You get the feeling sometimes it exists for novelty only, and on some week nights when less than a dozen patrons stare at each other, you might want to bring a good book. But come late on a Friday or Saturday night and the place will fill up with a friendly, predominately gay male clientele, with some gals too. Also light meals and *pupus* are served. 75-5660 Kopiko Street, Kailua–Kona. (808) 329-8558.

LODGING (LGBT)

ABSOLUTE PARADISE This gay male B&B is housed in a spiffy, modern house just a stroll away from Kehena nude beach in Puna. Their spacious rooms all have ocean views, with some having high-beamed ceilings, large picture windows, and private patio doors. The large pool, sundeck, and hot tub are always clothing-optional. Helpful owners Phil and Didier will assist you by pointing out great local secrets spots on the island, including trails to the active lava flows. (888) 285-1540, (808) 965-1828. ABSOLUTEPARADISE. TV **INEXPENSIVE, NUDIST-FRIENDLY**

ALOHA GUEST HOUSE A large two-story home run by JoHann, the friendly gay German host, this guesthouse is way up the mountainside with sweeping views of the South Kona coast. The large home works perfectly as a B&B, with lanais on both levels, large and medium guest rooms, and lots of peace and quiet. The upstairs bath sports an amazing two-headed shower and whirlpool bathtub room, big enough for you and all your friends! Good place for romantic seclusion. 84-4780 Mamalahoa Highway, Honaunau. (800) 897-3188, (808) 328-8955. ALOHAGUESTHOUSE.COM **MODERATE, PET-FRIENDLY, NUDIST-FRIENDLY**

BUTTERFLY INN A wonderfully secluded women-only B&B, the Butterfly Inn has been run for over a decade by the friendly Patti and Kay. Located about halfway between Hilo and the volcanoes, the house is on an acre lot, with a backyard bordering what used to be sugar cane fields. In the back you will find a hot outdoor shower, hot tub, and steam house with naturist sunbathing possible. There are two rooms upstairs, with common bath and kitchen. P.O. Box 6010, Kurtistown. (800) 54-MAGIC, (808) 966-7936. THEBUTTERFLYINN.COM **INEXPENSIVE, NUDIST-FRIENDLY**

HORIZON GUEST HOUSE This is a luxuriously tasteful bed and breakfast resort that offers miles of uninterrupted views of the huge Pacific on over 40 acres of upcountry land with goats and cattle. Features include an excellent Infinity pool and whirlpool, four classy rooms full of antique Asian furnishings, private lanais and bathrooms, and wonderful amenities like a laundry room and outside shower. Clem, the owner, custom-designed the whole property from scratch, and his vision shows through. First class all the way. P.O. Box 957, Honaunau. (888) 328-8301, (808) 328-2540. HORIZONGUESTHOUSE.COM **EXPENSIVE, KID-FRIENDLY, PET-FRIENDLY, HANDICAP-FRIENDLY, NUDIST-FRIENDLY**

KALANI OCEANSIDE RETREAT This well-known gay-popular retreat on Puna's coastline has a large hetero following as well. Bordering a lush and misty conservation area (the largest in Hawaii), the resort is fairly down-home and a bit basic for the comfort-loving (no phones nor TV). There is a pool and steam room, buffet-style vegetarian fair, and regular weeklong Body Electric Massage, Wild Women, and Pacific Men's Gathering workshops and retreats. Most of the staff lives on the property as part of a work program, and nudism takes over for particular events. RR 2, Box 4500-IP,

Kehena Beach, Pahoa. (800) 800-6866, (808) 965-7828. KALANI.
COM **MODERATE, NUDIST-FRIENDLY**

LODGING (MAINSTREAM)

HALE OHIA COTTAGES Gay-owned but with a predominantly straight clientele, this picturesque property is just a mile from Volcanoes National Park, set amid 60-year-old botanical gardens. There's one main lodge and adjoining cottages, one with a lava rock fireplace. A small, outdoor Japanese furo tub sits under Tsugi pines, and the rooms are personable and charming, complete with books and games. It gets a wee chilly here at night, lending to the coziness of it all. The gay owners will help you out with info about

HILO TOWN, UNDILUTED BY TOURISM

current lava viewing too. P.O. Box 758, Volcano. (800) 455-3803, (808) 967-7986. HALEOHIA.COM **MODERATE, KID-FRIENDLY, HANDICAP-FRIENDLY**

HILTON WAIKOLOA VILLAGE The mother of all Hawaiian resorts these 62 acres are a visual definition of the word *opulent*. You'll witness waterfalls plunging into swimming pools, water slides, a monorail system, a canal for passenger boats, gourmet restaurants, $5 million of Asian art (well, some are replicas), a wedding chapel, and a protected lagoon where you can pay to play with captive dolphins (if your name happens to get picked from a lottery). Amazingly, everything is open to the public, except the swimming pools. 69-425 Waikoloa Beach Drive, Waikoloa. (800) HILTONS, (808) 886-1234. HILTONWAIKOLOAVILLAGE.COM **EXPENSIVE, KID-FRIENDLY, HANDICAP-FRIENDLY**

FOUR SEASONS RESORT HUALALAI This understated, elegant, and secluded seaside bungalow resort is popular with Hollywood stars for a good reason: The five-star service is impeccable, the grounds are along the dramatic volcanic rock coast with seawater and fresh water swimming pools, and the award-winning open-air spa and health club is to die for. The hotel is complemented by a private Jack Nicklaus signature golf course, and the whole place feels like a luxurious private compound. 72-100 Kaupulehu Drive, Kaupulehu-Kona. (888) 340-5662, (808) 325-8000. FOURSEASONS. COM/HUALALAI **EXPENSIVE, KID-FRIENDLY, PET-FRIENDLY, HANDICAP-FRIENDLY**

VOLCANO HOUSE Although there may be fancier places to stay in the Big Island, none of them beat the cozy 42-room Volcano House's location right on the rim of the Halenaumau crater in the Volcanoes National Park. There's a restaurant offering excellent views down the crater, although afternoons tend to get foggy and almost cold up here. Check out the lobby fireplace that has been continuously burning for over 125 years! This mountain lodge, which evolved out of a grass lean-to in 1824, is Hawaii's oldest visitor accommodation. Stay only if you can get a room facing the volcano. Hawaii Volcanoes National Park. (808) 967-7321. VOLCANOHOUSEHOTEL.COM **MODERATE, KID-FRIENDLY, HANDICAP-FRIENDLY**

DINING

THE BAMBOO RESTAURANT The light, inventive meals prepared with fresh local products at Bamboo are a step above most of the tourist fare on the island. Located on the northern tip of the island in the old sugar town of Hawi, the restaurant is housed in a former hotel and dry goods store that dates from 1911. It's home to the best chicken pot stickers and babyback ribs in the state, served by gracious waitresses who often break into an impromptu hula right in the middle of a dining room that feels like an old Hawaiian tropical home. Off Highway 270 in Hawi. (808) 889-5555. BAMBOORESTAURANT.INFO **MODERATE**

CAFE PESTO An airy, comfortable bistro with ceiling fans and a black and white motif, and windows overlooking Hilo's historic waterfront. Light, California-style personal pizzas are served, with local toppings like kalua pork and Hamakua goat cheese, *poke* (Hawaiian-style sashimi), organic salads, and fresh fish dishes. The wait staff is some of the friendliest and most helpful you'll find in Hilo (although let's say the competition's not too fierce). 308 Kamehameha Avenue, Hilo. (808) 969-6640. CAFEPESTO.COM **MODERATE**

HUGGO'S For the quintessential Hawaiian seafood restaurant built over the ocean, Huggo's does not disappoint. Spotlights at night shine into the water, attracting fish and manta rays. There are nautical charts on the tabletops, a roomy open-air bar, and live local bands on most nights. The gay-owned restaurant has been in the same island family for over 30 years. Try the slow-roasted Black Angus prime rib, mahi mahi with prawns, or the outrageous Kona coffee mud pie—a three course meal in itself! 75-5828 Kahakai Road, Kailua–Kona. (808) 329-1493. HUGGOS.COM **EXPENSIVE**

MERRIMAN'S A longtime favorite restaurant on the Big Island that most tourists would simply drive past, Merriman's is something of a culinary legend. It's located in the ranch town of Waimea and chef/owner Peter Merriman is a three-time finalist in the James Beard Awards for Best Chef, Pacific Northwest and Hawaii. The cuisine is freshly-grown from the surrounding area, and the menu is constantly changing based on seasonality, and includes yummies like crispy lamb spring rolls, grilled Big Island strip loin, and sautéed Waimea spinach. Opelo Road and Highway 19, Waimea. (808) 885-6822. MERRIMANSHAWAII.COM **EXPENSIVE**

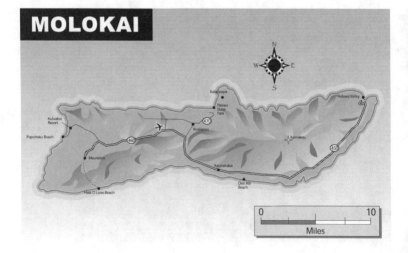

ISLAND FACTS

MOLOKAI IS NICKNAMED: "The Friendly Isle"

ISLAND COLOR: Green

ISLAND FLOWER: White *Kukui* Blossom

LAND MASS: 260 sq. miles/676 sq. km

POPULATION: 7,000 est.

HIGHEST POINT: Kamakou at 4,961 feet/1,512 m

RAINFALL: 27 inches/69 cm at the Molokai Airport

Molokai has Hawaii's highest named waterfall, Kahiwa, at 1,750 feet. Some of the world's highest sea cliffs are on the island's north shore at 3,300 feet with a 58-degree slope. The world's largest rubber-lined reservoir is near Kualapuu, holding 1.4 billion gallons of water.

GEOGRAPHICAL OVERVIEW

Even the word *town* might be stretching it for the island's main center of **KAUNAKAKAI**. If you blink you'll miss it, even if you're walking. The settlement has the distinct feeling of old rural Hawaii. A quaint town wharf is near town, where teenagers hang out, ships unload, and the foundation remains of King Kamehameha V's vacation house sit nearby. If you stand at the main intersection of Highway 460 and Ala Malama Street, you'll spot the tourist information office on your right. Ala Malama curves around to the main drag into the heart of Kaunakakai, which lasts a whole whopping three blocks, complete with aged western storefronts housing a few stores and restaurants. A must-stop is the '50s-style Kanemitsu Bakery, which bakes the famous Molokai bread. The bakery also has a very local coffee shop that serves sandwiches and breakfast, with tacky painted murals of hula girls and a large relief map hanging on the wall.

From Kaunakakai, head east toward the airport on Highway 460. You will spot the 10-acre **KAPUAIWA COCONUT GROVE** just one mile from town, one of Hawaii's last surviving royal groves. Across the highway is another enchanted sight, **CHURCH ROW**, where various denominations were given a plot of land to set up shop right next to one another, side by side like reverent dominos. As the highway begins to climb up from the dry grasslands, continue on to Highway 470 and make a left on 480 into the micro-town of **KUALAPUU**. The town was built by the Del Monte Corporation, who ran the pineapple plantations here until pulling out in the early '80s. The area is now trying its hand at coffee. Further up the road is the **KUALAPUU COOKHOUSE** (*see Dining*), and further still is the arid, spread-out community of Hoolehua, known for its ethnic Hawaiian population living on homestead lands.

Back on Highway 470 heading north, the scenery becomes a bit greener. You will soon pass the **MEYER SUGAR MILL**, with a century-old steam engine and displays on Molokai's history. Further up are pasturelands and then the road ends at **PALAAU STATE PARK**, a 200 plus acre reserve. One trail here leads to the **KALAUPAPA OVERLOOK**, where you gawk across the sheer cliffs to the leper colony of Kalaupapa below. The other trail leads up a wooded hill to the **PHALLIC ROCK (KAULEONANAHOA)** in a little clearing within an ironwood grove. The shape of the rock looks like it's been helped out by human hands a little. It has been said that women who spend the night here could become pregnant.

One thing the visitor to Molokai should really do is visit the **LEPROSY COLONY OF KALAUPAPA**, one of the most soul-stirring journeys you can take in Hawaii. A vertical, switchback hike down to the peninsula takes about an hour and a half, but it's a lot more fun to join one of the mule tours (there are also short flights down). Any way you get there, you must hook up with **DAMIEN TOURS** to be able to see the colony, who take you around the colony by a school bus and give you the lowdown.

The quiet village holds fewer than 100 generally elderly people. Most are technically afflicted with leprosy, which is now called Hansen's Disease and is treatable by sulfone drugs and not contagious. For decades, the sick were forced to swim from offshore boats and fend for themselves at this remote outpost, completely disowned by family and burying each other in unmarked graves. The four-hour tour includes a stop by **FATHER DAMIEN'S CHURCH**, named after the selfless Belgian priest who built the entire thing by himself while living with the lepers, then died of leprosy in 1889.

OUT TRAVELER RATINGS GUIDE

GAY-FRIENDLY: ▼▼▼
GAY SCENE: ▼
LESBIAN SCENE: --
PRO-GAY LAWS: ▼▼▼
HIV RESOURCES: ▼▼▼

From 470, backtrack and turn west on 460 toward the airport. You'll see the slumbering **MAUNALOA MOUNTAIN RANGE** where the goddess Laka is said to have learned how to dance, giving birth to the hula. The highway ends amid cattle land and the old Dole pineapple plantation town of **MAUNALOA**. The town borders the nearby Molokai Ranch, and investment by the owners include a town facelift of ranch-like wooden buildings, a paved road, cute shops (including the fascinating Big Wind Kite Factory, selling artistic kites), the island's only movie theater, and yes, a Kentucky Fried Chicken! The spiffy town is also trying to attract an upcountry residential population with rows of quaint rustic homes.

Before you reach the end of 460, you will find the turn-off at the 15 mile marker for the **KALUAKOI RESORT AREA**. This is the island's only "touristy" spot, which still isn't saying much. A few hotels and condos and a golf course dot the lovely Kepuhi Beach. South of the Kaluakoi Resort along Kaluakoi Road is **PAPOHAKU BEACH**. This vast white stretch of beauty is one of Hawaii's longest and most deserted beaches. Calm summer days are better for swimming, since the wind can get intense and there are rocky outcrops. The empty Papohaku offers some small sand dunes in the back, which could be used for some discreet nude sunning, since there are few footprints on the sand, even on busy days.

Making your way back to Kaunakakai town again, head east on Kamehameha V Highway (450). You'll pass island homes along the shore, with views of fisherman knee-deep in water throwing nets along the shallow mud flats. There are a number of beach parks on this road, good for picnicking and viewing the island of Lanai. A few miles later on the right hand side of the road is a sweet one-room church built by Father Damien called **ST. JOSEPH'S**, with an unflattering statue of the father and a quiet graveyard.

Keep a careful eye out to the coast, since you will see a number of rock-walled aquaculture fishponds along the highway. The adept Hawaiians built them in order to have a constant supply of fish.

The road quickly turns into blind curves as you pass popular surf spots around rocky points, with views of Kahana Rock off the coast. The highway will begin to head upwards and become more forested as you approach the jungled **HALAWA VALLEY**. This lush gorge is home to waterfalls and after it was hit by two tsunamis in the 1940s and 1950s, only a handful of permanent families live here. It makes a picturesque end to the island.

MOLOKAI'S NORTH SHORE, HOME OF THE WORLD'S HIGHEST SEA CLIFFS

GAY TRAVELER OF HAWAII YESTERYEAR

An interesting footnote in American literature is the story
of writer and poet Charles Warren Stoddard. A one-time
secretary to Mark Twain and devoted pen pal to Walt
Whitman and Herman Melville, this "Boy Poet of San
Francisco" in 1864 at the age of 21 took off to Hawaii for
adventure. He found much more than he bargained for.

Corresponding with Mr. Whitman, he explained that
among the islands he could act out his "nature" in a way
he couldn't "even in California, where men are tolerably
bold." Stoddard had not only fallen in love with Hawaii's
beauty and culture, but with many "coffee-colored,"
frequently nude teenage boys. His descriptions of rapturous
evenings spent with island youths fill his stories with
blatant homoeroticism, like passages from this story about a
visit to Molokai in 1869:

> "I was taken in, fed, and petted in every possible
> way, and finally put to bed, where Kana–ana
> monopolized me, growling in true savage fashion
> if anyone came near. I didn't sleep much, after all.
> I must have been excited."

and:

> "Again and again, he would come with a
> delicious banana to the bed where I was lying,

and insist upon my gorging myself … He would
mesmerize me into a most refreshing sleep with a
prolonged and pleasing manipulation."

Although racy enough to make modern readers blush, in
the 1800s homosexual escapades were not even considered
a valid reality, and many critics brushed Stoddard's work
off as colorful and even silly. Although a devoted Catholic,
Stoddard traveled a number of times to Hawaii and Tahiti to
fall in love with "untrammeled youths," calling them by the
intimate phrase "*aikane*—bosom friend."

In the autobiographical story, "Chumming with a
Savage," which took place in one of Molokai's lush
north shore valleys, Stoddard slips out in the middle
of the night by canoe, only to have his "little sea–god"
Kana–ana rushing madly after him, completely naked in
the waves, calling out his name. Stoddard's tropical affairs
were passionate and earnest, but usually ill-fated. Thus,
homosexual life in the 1800s.

Stoddard also became friends with Father Damien
and wrote a book about him, *The Lepers of Molokai*,
which helped make the father a well-known figure. For
a fascinating glimpse into gay old Hawaii, a collection of
Stoddard's stories, long out of print, has been republished
as *Cruising the South Seas* by Gay Sunshine Press in San
Francisco.

OVERVIEW OF THE SCENE
AND SCENESTERS

Visiting Molokai is like stepping into a time machine. This is not the
place for glamorous parties or fancy shops: Unhurried farmers and
horses easily outnumber the tourists on any given day. The people
here talk slow and drive slow since there's tons of Hawaiian Time
for everything. Besides the island of Niihau, Molokai's residents
have the highest percentage of Hawaiian blood than on any other
island. Residents take pride in the fact that there are no traffic lights
on the island, and no building is taller than a palm tree. If you
want to see how Hawaii was, and perhaps was meant to be, then
Molokai's the place to head.

At first glance, there seems nothing queer at all about this rural
island. But little Molokai is not only known, but renowned for its
resident transvestites, simply called *mahu*. Many live and work in
drag, being accepted for who they are, and are affectionately called
Auntie or Tutu. *Mahu* tend to be unassuming rather than flashy in
small-town Molokai, but it's hard to get across the island without
bumping into one. They often work as wait help at the restaurants.
By far they are at the forefront of the hula renaissance on the island,
which many traditions say is the birthplace of hula. They stage local
performances and win awards internationally.

The resident *mahu* on Molokai are usually quite friendly
despite the Molokaians' wariness of outsiders. The local populace is
completely respectful toward the *mahu*, since they are an acceptable
way to be "gay" here, and many *mahu* are integral members of the
family. In fact, there are stories of certain Molokai police officers
settling down and setting up house with *mahu*. Talk about approval!

Popular pastimes on quiet Molokai are cock-fighting, taro
growing, and of course "talking story," since unemployment here
is some of the highest in the state. New industries like coffee and

eco-tourism on Molokai Ranch are being developed to curb the unemployment rate.

Molokai was left on its own for a good portion of its history, perhaps due in part to stories of famous sorcerers who resided here. They were said to have carved poisonwood idols and concocted incantations to keep visitors at bay. Nowadays the residents are a tad more friendly, although perhaps not always as kissy-feely to tourists as the island's motto will have you believe. Don't forget you are a guest on this island, one of the least developed and least touristy in the chain.

TO DO AND SEE

THE MOLOKAI MULE RIDE This classic island outing into the old leper colony of Kalaupapa is, despite the steep price, the traditional tourist outing on the island. You sit on an ass as it makes its way down 1,700 feet of perilous cliffs and precarious switchbacks to the quiet village, where you board a Damien Tour bus and see the sights. Molokai without the mule rides is like San Francisco without the cable cars. (800) 567-7550, (808) 567-6088. MULERIDE.COM

PANIOLO ROUNDUP A cattle roundup in a fully equipped rodeo arena? It's not what you'd expect from a Hawaiian vacation, making this outing through the Molokai Ranch even more special. Real *paniolos* (cowboys) teach you how to round up cattle and the finer points or horsemanship and rodeo games during a half-day, real-life adventure. (888) 627-8082, MOLOKAIRANCH.COM

LODGING (MAINSTREAM)

HOTEL MOLOKAI This nostalgic (for the 1970s at least) yet upgraded Hawaiian motel complex is composed of a series of modified A-frame units, nestled under coco palms along Kamiloloa

Beach, adjacent to Hawaii's only barrier reef. The hotel has a pool and bar/restaurant, and rooms are fairly basic (be sure to ask for one with a ceiling fan), but cheerful, with kitchenettes and lanais. But it's the only choice if you want to stay in the centralized area of Kaunakakai. Kamehameha V Highway, Kaunakakai. 808-553-5347. HOTELMOLOKAI.COM **MODERATE, HANDICAP-FRIENDLY, KID-FRIENDLY**

THE LODGE AT MOLOKAI RANCH On the western end of the island fronting Kaupoa Beach are 22 luxury rooms and 40 canvas two-bedroom "tentalows" (with full bathrooms) amid the 65,000 acres of ranchland (with a nearby 18-hole golf course). If you're staying in the luxury tents, hang out in hammocks on the

SAINT PHILOMENA CHURCH IN KALAWAO, MOLOKAI, DATES TO 1872

humanless beach while your shower is heated by solar energy, and if it all feels too much like roughing it, head to the lodge's bar and restaurant for a full buffet. A true Hawaiian experience either way. 100 Maunaloa Highway, Maunaloa. (888) 627-8082, (808) 660-2824. MOLOKAIRANCH.COM **EXPENSIVE, PET-FRIENDLY, HANDICAP-FRIENDLY, KID-FRIENDLY**

DINING

MAUNALOA ROOM Molokai is not where you head for fine dining, but the Lodge at Molokai Ranch comes pretty close with its upscale eatery. With emphasis on fresh Molokai ingredients and inventive island dishes like banana-stuffed Molokai sweetbread French toast, eggs with taro hash, and Hawaiian snapper with tropical-fruit salsa and ginger lime butter. Hawaiian proverbs are stenciled on to the walls, and the open-air views make you want to linger. 100 Maunaloa Highway, Maunaloa. (888) 627-8082, (808) 660-2824. MOLOKAIRANCH.COM **EXPENSIVE**

KUALAPUU COOKHOUSE You'll know this down-home country restaurant by the wagon in the front, and by its wooden tables and benches, cowbells, yokes, and hand plows adorning the walls. At one time the cafeteria for the Del Monte plantation, the cookhouse now calls itself the headquarters of "the slow food chain." The menu has specialty omelettes, mahi mahi burgers, homemade tropical chili, ribs, and chocolate macadamia nut pie. Patio seating is on the side, and the indoor pane windows look out onto the countryside. Farrington Highway 1 block west of Highway 470, Kalapuu. (808) 567-9655

LANAI

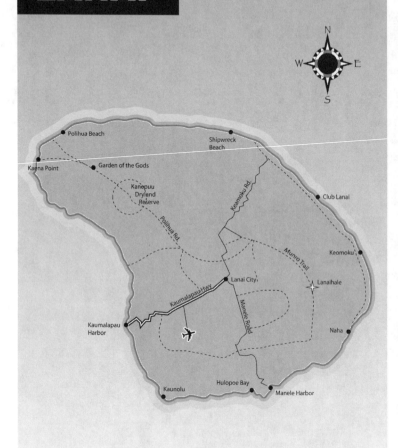

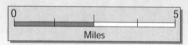

Miles

0   5

ISLAND FACTS

LANAI IS NICKNAMED: "The Pineapple Island"

ISLAND COLOR: Orange

ISLAND FLOWER: Kaunaoa

LAND MASS: 141 sq. miles/367 sq. km

POPULATION: 3,200 est.

HIGHEST POINT: Lainaihale at 3,366 feet/1,026 m

RAINFALL: 37 inches/94 cm in Lanai City, 12 inches/30 cm on most coasts

GEOGRAPHICAL OVERVIEW

Calling microscopic **LANAI CITY** a "city" is the biggest misnomer you'll find in Hawaii. However, this is where almost all of Lanai's population resides in trim multi-colored plantation-style blocks, amidst huge Norfolk and Cook Island pines. The mood is of a peaceful, rustic mountain town. This tidy upland village becomes cool and misty in the afternoons and is so unhurried and mellow that shops even close for a noontime siesta. A grid of streets surround the main center of town, **DOLE PARK**. Around the park, a handful of idyllic shops and eateries face the grass. This is where you'll find all of the isle's restaurants, shops, movie theater, school, post office, and churches.

The road south out of Lanai City to **MANELE BAY** is a nice smooth piece of pavement that only takes 20 minutes from start to finish. You will pass the wide fields that were once chock-full of pineapple, and after you descend down the open hillside, views of uninhabited Kahoolawe Island appear on the horizon.

The first major right is the site of the posh **MANELE BAY HOTEL** (*see Lodging*) with an adjoining golf course. After that you will see the cliffs surrounding **MANELE BOAT HARBOR**, where scuba and snorkel boats and the ferry to Maui leave from. The road soon loops around at the popular **HULOPOE BEACH PARK**, a white sandy beach with Lanai's best snorkeling and swimming in crystal waters, tucked away in a cove with the resort watching over.

Backtracking to Lanai City, take the rougher Highway 44 north out of town. You can't miss the **LODGE AT KOELE** (*see Lodging*) on your right. A mile past the lodge is a paved road on the right, which will take you to a colorful Filipino cemetery with brightly decorated tombstones, and then the road quickly becomes dirt and turns into the **MUNRO TRAIL**. The red potholed road rocks its way through thick foliage and pines, past views of the encircling neighbor islands and the ocean beyond. You feel like you are miles away from any form of civilization. The trail ultimately descends back down to the highway, passing some petroglyphs on the way.

Further on Highway 44, past the turn–off for the Munro Trail, the road floats past horses in green pastures and then descends to the dry rugged coastline. Right after the paved road ends near the coast, take the sharp left fork for the dirt road to **SHIPWRECK BEACH**. You can't really swim here, but the view of the tilted cargo ship rusting away offshore makes an interesting souvenir photo.

If you turn around and head southeast along the coastal dirt road, you will see great views of Maui and 5 miles later, the ghost town of **KEOMUKU**. All that really remains of the failed sugar venture here is an empty wooden church house dating back to 1903, now maintained by volunteers. Look inside at the sweet altar where people leave cash offerings.

Further down the dusty road is a small jetty for **CLUB LANAI**. Appearing as a bizarre oasis amid all the dry abandoned scrub, a boat drops Maui tourists off at this remote spot for kayaking, and sunbathing. The dirt road goes further down the parched coast to the desolate and empty fishing spot of Naha.

Back at the Lodge at Koele, there's a dirt road leading to the west just past the resort with a sign for Garden of the Gods on your left. Red dust flies around you as you head northwest to the fenced-in **KANEPUU DRYLAND RESERVE**, some of the last remaining Hawaiian dry lands not devastated by wild goats and cattle. There are a couple of marked trails if you feel like wandering.

Right after you exit the reserve's gate, you will begin to spot the weird rock formations that make up the **GARDEN OF THE GODS**. You'll immediately wonder why it's called a garden. The sparse, eerie landscape that stretches all the way down the mountainside has ghostly rock configurations and stacks in hues of red and beige,

OUT TRAVELER RATINGS GUIDE

GAY-FRIENDLY: ▼▼

GAY SCENE: --

LESBIAN SCENE: --

PRO-GAY LAWS: ▼▼▼

HIV RESOURCES: ▼▼

with the bright blue of the ocean as a contrasting backdrop. Keep your eyes peeled in this whole region for the famous Lanai Axis Deer.

The dirt road will have a major fork soon, with signs for either Kaena Point or Polihua Beach. The descending road to the beach feels more like a jagged empty creek bed, complete with boulders and gullies. How driveable it is depends on whether they have cleared the road lately.

If you make it to the **POLIHUA BEACH**, you'll find an amazingly wide, windswept piece of sand devoid of people, making for a perfect nude picnic spot. If you take the Kaena Point fork instead, you would bump and grind all the way to some dark sea cliffs on the northwest shore, with some heiau remains nearby.

OVERVIEW OF THE SCENE AND SCENESTERS

Lanai is a small dry island in Maui's rain shadow, with only a couple of major resorts, a picturesque village-town, a mere 30 miles of paved roads, and no traffic lights to be had. For centuries, Hawaiians avoided the place because of stories of evil spirits that dwelled here. It wasn't until a mischievous son of one of Maui's kings was sent to Lanai and killed all the evil spirits that people began to populate the island.

Lanai holds an old organized plantation feel to it, ever since Jim Dole bought the whole darn thing in the early 1920s for a little over $1 million to grow pineapples. The Castle & Cooke Company still owns 98% of the island. Pineapple production was phased out in the early 1990s, but the company eased the majority of the island's Filipino-dominated population into the tourist era with the construction of two mega-luxury resorts, not to mention three golf courses. Some call the company too paternalistic, but with subsidized rent, high wages, and a wealthy visitor base, Lanai has a somewhat brighter economic outlook than many other parts of the state.

Despite its patina of luxury, Lanai is really made for the adventurous. The one and only rental car company offers four-wheel drive jeeps and maps to remote beaches on the northern coast, the forested spine of the Munro Trail, and the Garden of the Gods. You'll be coated by the island's red dust by the end of it, but you will be rewarded by having a glimpse of an old, interesting island many tourists never get to explore.

You can also do day trips from Maui via the 60-passenger ferry *Expeditions* out of Lahaina, offering whale and dolphin sightings in the process.

TO DO AND SEE

THE EXPERIENCE AT KOELE Golf is a major diversion on quiet Lanai, and this upcountry par-72 championship course designed by golf legend Greg Norman and architect Ted Robinson, offers stunning views of the island. It begins on a 2,000-foot elevation plateau with wooded ravines, seven lakes, streams, and cascading waterfalls. Its signature hole, Number 17, plays from a 250-foot elevated tee squeezed between a lake on one side and dense foliage the other. The front nine move dramatically through the entire course. The best part is relaxing in the ultra-chic clubhouse at the Lodge at Koele hotel afterwards. (808) 565-4000. **EXPENSIVE** FOURSEASONS.COM/KOELE

LODGING (MAINSTREAM)

HOTEL LANAI Dating back to 1923, this old-time lodge has quite a homey feel to it, with hardwood floors, pedestal sinks, a few four-poster beds, and patchwork quilts. Ask for one of the rooms with porches in front at no extra cost, overlooking pine-filled Lanai City. There's a quite decent country restaurant, and it's the reasonably priced place to stay, especially considering breakfast is included as is a complimentary snorkel equipment. (800) 795-7211, (808) 565-7211. HOTELLANAI.COM **MODERATE, HANDICAP-FRIENDLY, KID-FRIENDLY**

MANELE BAY HOTEL This luxe hotel's 250 luxury Mediterranean villas and suites with private lanais offer incredible views of the sparkling Hulopoe Beach. There's a dark wood library with leather-bound books and chess boards, a comfortable if ritzy Asian-motif lobby with deep couches, painted murals, sculptures, and vases, a number of theme gardens, and tons of Italian marble everywhere, including the suite's bathrooms. An all-out spa and exercise center

MANELE BOAT HARBOR, LANAI

beckons, and the nearby 18-hole oceanfront golf course was designed by Jack Nicklaus. If all this isn't enough, butler suites are also available. (808) 565-2000. FOURSEASONS.COM/MANELEBAY

EXPENSIVE, HANDICAP-FRIENDLY, KID-FRIENDLY

THE LODGE AT KOELE Appearing like a transplanted English manor house, this Four Seasons property is for those who don't need to be near the beach and want to experience one of the most distinctively tasteful resorts in the state. Deluxe suites with verandahs overlook the perfectly manicured lawns where croquet, lawn bowling, and miniature golf are played. The grand lobby called the Great Hall is sumptuous with dark, rich wood, skylights, soft couches, objets d'art, and the two largest stone fireplaces in Hawaii, not to mention lovely reading and sitting rooms in the wings that will make you feel like a hunter coming in for rest. (808) 565-4000. FOURSEASONS.COM/KOELE **EXPENSIVE, HANDICAP-FRIENDLY**

DINING

DINING ROOM AT THE LODGE AT KO'ELE Open only for dinner, this lush 60-seat restaurant offers sumptuous comfort in its tall wooden chairs, soothing live piano music, roaring fireplace, and views out into the large pond and dark green lawns. The menu features estate-grown ingredients, with an emphasis on local fish and game. You might want to head to the Terrace Dining Room for afternoon British high tea as well. Either way, everyone dresses up for the expensive but justified prices. (808) 565-4000. FOURSEASONS. COM/KOELE **EXPENSIVE**

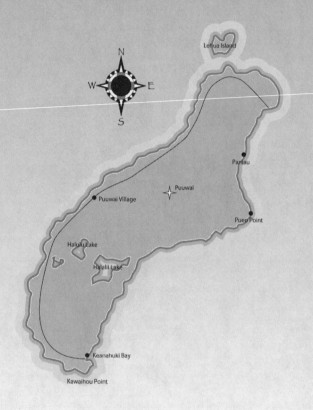

NIIHAU

Kaulakahi Channel

Lehua Island

N
W   E
S

Paniau

Puuwai

Puuwai Village

Pueo Point

Halulu Lake

Halalii Lake

Keanahuki Bay

Kawaihou Point

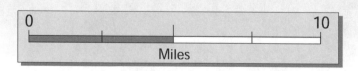

0   10

Miles

ISLAND FACTS

NIIHAU IS NICKNAMED: "The Forbidden Island"
ISLAND COLOR: White
ISLAND FLOWER: Pupu
LAND MASS: 70 sq. miles/180 sq. km
POPULATION: 160 est.
HIGHEST POINT: Paniau at 1,250 feet/381 m
RAINFALL: 19 inches/48 cm

The only island on earth where Hawaiian is spoken as a first language, and the smallest of Hawaii's seven inhabited islands. Site of Hawaii's largest lake, Halalii, at 841 to 865 acres (depending on rainfall).

GEOGRAPHICAL OVERVIEW

The north shore of Niihau looks out onto the uninhabited crescent-shaped **LEHUA ISLAND**. On the island's northwest shore is **KEAWANUI**, a stunning 3.5 mile stretch of beach. A lot of Niihau women spend time creating the intricate **NIIHAU LEI NECKLACES** from seashells washed ashore on the island's beaches. The delicate jewelry is coveted throughout Hawaii. The one main dirt road on the island runs along the island's western spine, where Niihau's main village **PUUWAI** sits about midpoint. The town is the center of the island's ranching operations, with stone walls built up around the houses to keep out the grazing animals. South of Puuwai are two large lakes, **HALULU** and **HALALII**, which can dry up to puddles during rough droughts. The dirt road ends at **KEANAHAKI BAY** on the southern tip of the island.

OVERVIEW OF THE SCENE AND SCENESTERS

This arid, desert isle 18 miles off the western coast of Kauai is as intriguing as it is mysterious. Bought by Elizabeth Sinclair in 1864 for $10,000 from King Kamehameha IV and completely controlled by the Robinson family ever since, life on Niihau is simple and untamed. There are no airports, no telephones, no restaurants, no movie theaters, no paved roads, and relatively few trucks or cars. Everyone is employed by the Robinson's cattle ranch, so rent is unnecessary.

The catch to all this quaint tranquility (and it's a whopper) is that no outsiders are allowed to visit Niihau. It is completely closed off to non-residents, save for restricted helicopter flights to specific uninhabited spots. Hence its nickname "The Forbidden Island." Residents of Niihau, a majority of who are full-blooded Hawaiian, are allowed to visit the other islands, but cannot bring anyone back to Niihau with them. When a Niihauan marries an outsider, they are rarely allowed to return. This compound-like system means a dwindling population due to younger people leaving for more modern lifestyles. But the exclusive paternalism (some say dictatorship) of the Robinson family has allowed for a uniquely Hawaiian culture to flourish, far from the over-paving and commercialism of other parts of the state. The only way for non-residents to see the island is via pricey helicopter tours that land but stay far away from inhabited areas, or by boat tours that cruise along its coast.

The Robinson ranch could obviously make a better profit by selling the island outright, for assumingly a bit more than the $10,000 they paid for it. They have evaded this option despite grave financial concerns due to extremely high taxes imposed by the state. A potential deal with the U.S. Navy to expand its missle launching facilities on Niihau fell through in the 1990s. Whether this last outpost of Hawaiiana will survive the twenty-first century completely unscathed, or succumb to modern market pressures, is anyone's guess.

TO DO AND SEE

HOLO HOLO CHARTERS At 65 feet, *Holo Holo* is Kauai's largest vessel, a catamaran that takes 49 passengers to discover the forbidden isle of Niihau. Departing from Hanapepe Bay of Kauai, they offer full day tours that take in both the dramatically carved Na Pali Coast on Kauai's northern shore, as well as a snorkel spot on rarely-visited Niihau. Food, drinks, and equipment are included. (800) 848-6130, (808) 335-0815. HOLOHOLOCHARTERS.COM

NIIHAU HELICOPTERS AND SAFARIS This is the only company offering flight tours of Niihau, taking off from Kauai on a twin-engine helicopter. Depending on the weather, the chopper lands at two sites, a beach on the north shore and Keanahaki Bay in the south, avoiding Puuwai where people live. Snacks are provided on the half-day tours, which allow you to beach comb at remote spots. The company also hosts full-day hunting tours for sheep and wild boar. (877) 441-3500. NIIHAU.US.

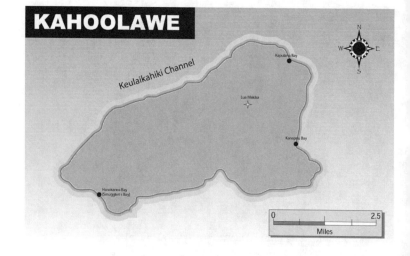

KAHOOLAWE

Keulaikahiki Channel

Kapueihi Bay

Lua Makika

Kanapou Bay

Hanakanaia Bay
(Smuggler's Bay)

0   2.5
Miles

ISLAND FACTS

KAHOOLAWE IS NICKNAMED: "The Uninhabited Island"
ISLAND COLOR: Gray
ISLAND FLOWER: Hinahina
LAND MASS: 45 sq. miles/117 sq. km
POPULATION: 0
HIGHEST POINT: Lua Makika 1,477 feet/450 m
RAINFALL: 15 inches/38 cm

The only uninhabited of Hawaii's eight major islands, and the only one ever solely used for military target practice.

GEOGRAPHICAL OVERVIEW

Kahoolawe's shape looks something like the profile of a crouching lion gazing east. The island's slopes, once a little greener, have been meticulously eaten away to a dusty brown by goats and sheep during the ranching days. Wild goats were finally eradicated in 1993, but field mice and cats still wreak havoc over the ecosystem. Soil preservation has been a main concern for the future, and efforts at replanting native species have taken place.

KAULANA BAY on the northeast shore was the site of an encampment for exiled prisoners in the 1800s. On the island's southwest corner is **HANAKANEA BAY**, commonly known as Smuggler's Bay, since this is where smugglers used to hide illegal Chinese opium from the government. It's also been used as a military encampment as well.

OVERVIEW OF THE SCENE AND SCENESTERS

Kahoolawe has always been shrouded in dread. It's been said that the god Kanaloa ruled the land of the dead from this island, and in the old days the island was revered by dark sorcerers. Hawaiians inhabited the island in various phases throughout its history, but the isle's aridity and frequent droughts kept it from being a major population center. Kahoolawe was used as a male penal colony and place of exile from around 1830 to 1853, and prisoners reportedly starved, with some swimming across the channel to Maui to find food. A few mostly unsuccessful ranching efforts took over the island (destroying most of its native vegetation) until 1941, when the U.S. military confiscated the Kahoolawe after the bombing of Pearl Harbor. It was then used as a military bombing target site up until 1990, when President George Bush ended the practice.

However, the damage had already been done: it's been said that Kahoolawe was the most bombed island in the entire Pacific during World War II, and the military even simulated an atomic blast here. The final halting of the bombing was thanks in large part to the efforts of Hawaiian activist groups in the 1970s, who acted up and formed the Protect Kaho'olawe Ohana group, which advocated for the return of the island from the military. At times the group illegally occupied the island for demonstrations.

Their efforts paid off in 1980 when the Navy agreed to preserve the over 2,000 recorded archeological features on the island. Even though Kahoolawe was added to the National Register of Historic Places in 1981, the bombing continued until 1990. In 1994, during a moving service that included Hawaiian chants and prayers, the Navy relinquished rights to the island and returned it to the state of Hawaii. The island has since become a potent symbol for Hawaiian autonomy. In November 2003, the Navy's $400 million dollar clean-up of unexploded ordnance was officially over, although a good amount of it still exists. Nowadays, access to Kahoolawe is denied to all except government officials and members of the Protect Kahoolawe Ohana, who are involved with restoration efforts on the island. There are no paved roads, no ports, no airfields, and no inhabitants on the island. Future plans for a cultural reserve are being discussed, but it may be many, many moons from now.

BIBLIOGRAPHY

Kane, Herb Kawainui, *Pele: Goddess of Hawaii's Volcanoes.* Captain Cook, HI: The Kawainui Press, 1987.

Kalakaua, King David, *The Legends and Myths of Hawaii.* 1888.

Kay, Joshua (editor), *Pocket Guide to Hawaii.* Honolulu: Pacific Ocean Holidays, 1998.

McMahon, Richard, *Camping Hawaii: A Complete Guide.* Honolulu, University of Hawaii Press, 1994.

Malo, David, *Moolelo Hawaii* (Hawaiian Antiquities). Nathaniel B. Emerson, translator. 1898. Honolulu: Bishop Museum Press, 1976.

Maugham, W. Somerset, *The Trembling of a Leaf.* Honolulu: Mutual Publishing, 1990.

Pukui, Mary Kawena and Samuel H. Elbert, *New Pocket Hawaiian Dictionary.* Honolulu: University of Hawaii Press, 1992.

Morris, Robert J., Aikane: "Accounts of Same-Sex Relationships in the Journals of Captain Cook's Third Voyage." *Journal of Homosexuality,* Volume 19(4), The Haworth Press, 1990.

Reyes, Luis, *Made in Paradise: Hollywood's Films of Hawaii and the South Seas.* Honolulu: Mutual Publishing, 1995.

Stoddard, Charles Warren (edited by Winston Leyland), *Cruising the South Seas.* San Francisco: Gay Sunshine Press, 1987.

Tregaskis, Richard, *The Warrior King: Hawaii's Kamehameha the Great.* Honolulu: Falmouth Press, 1973.

Westervelt, William D., *Hawaiian Historical Legends.* Rutland, VT: Charles S. Tuttle, 1977.

INDEX